Pregnancy Center
East

4760 Madison Road
Cincinnati, OH 45227

513-321-3100

information@pregnancycentereast.com
www.PregnancyCenterEast.com

*Compliments
of PC Plus!*

Enjoy!

ENDORSEMENTS

"*Redeemed* is a courageously told story of Toni McFadden's journey to find healing and hope in Christ. Toni's bravery to share her tragic abortion experience and the redemption she later found is truly inspiring. In *Redeemed*, Toni takes us into the most painful moments of her life, exposing her past in hopes of sparing others the sorrow she endured. This book gives readers the strength to look at their own moments of pain and seek God that He would "work them all together for good" as Romans 8:28 promises. Toni is a woman of wisdom, honor, and integrity and that shines through the pages of this book. Redeemed is a testament to the faithfulness of God and a story you will want to share with others!"

— **CHRISTINA BENNETT**, SPEAKER, WRITER, AND NEWS CORRESPONDENT FOR LIVE ACTION

"Toni's powerful story of redemption, so vulnerably shared, is a needed testament to God's mercy and how He pursues and leads us. Her life experience from ashes to beauty is a mighty example proving that God is a Waymaker who parts the waters and makes a path from bondage to freedom."

— **STEPHANIE GRAY CONNORS**, SPEAKER AND AUTHOR, LOVE UNLEASHES LIFE

"Toni's story is heartbreaking, beautiful, and powerful. She vulnerably dives into the gut-wrenching aspects of what it's really like to have an abortion. She brings light to the fact that what the world sells as female empowerment leaves women empty, hurting, and opens the possibility of incredibly dangerous life-threatening side effects. Abortion is dark, but Toni reminds us that darkness doesn't have to be forever. It's not easy to share the most personal parts of your life, but by doing so, Toni will change hearts and minds and help women find the healing they've been searching for."

— **CHRISTINE YEARGIN,** SPEAKER, PRO-LIFE ADVOCATE, AND FOUNDER OF BE THEIR VILLAGE

"Toni McFadden is the ideological equivalent of Harriet Tubman, seeking to lift the spell on black America and the entire abortion industry. Toni shares her journey from the valley of the shadow of death to the light of life, from abortion to renewal. You can only take people where you've been, and Toni's journey will help encourage anyone lost from the tragedy of abortion to find their way back to the garden."

— **SETH GRUBER,** PRO-LIFE SPEAKER, AND THE HOST OF UNABORTED WITH SETH GRUBER PODCAST

TONI MCFADDEN

Redeemed

MY JOURNEY AFTER ABORTION

DEDICATION PAGE

To every woman who regrets their abortion and may be suffering in silence, this book is for you. May the words on these pages help you to see that healing is available and redemption is always within your reach.

THANK YOU PAGE

I want to first thank Jesus. For only He could bless me with this beautiful testimony to share with the world for His glory. Without the saving work of Jesus Christ, I would not have a story to tell.

I want to thank my incredible husband for encouraging me to go beyond what I think I can do. Thank you, Love, for seeing what I often cannot see in myself and for inspiring me to share our story. God has continued to show His grace and mercy on our lives, and I am so thankful my heart was preserved for you. I love you!

To those who walked alongside me in my healing, "Thank you." Your contributions, big and small, have changed my life and allowed me to support other people.

TABLE OF CONTENTS

FOREWORD

In November 2019, I was invited to speak in Puebla, Mexico, at a conference called, "The Epic Debate: The City of Ideas." Toni McFadden was there as a speaker as well. She shared her incredibly personal story in such a heartfelt, honest way. I recognized the courage it must have taken for her to begin speaking about her journey and was impressed by her bravery. We gained the opportunity to talk further when we were backstage, which allowed us to connect further. Toni's vivacious energy and passion were refreshing in someone so young. I happily invited her to stay in touch, and for the past few years, we have had the opportunity to get to know one another.

Toni's *Redeemed: My Journey after Abortion* is a story that is vitally necessary to our society. Toni candidly shares her experience with her own abortion and the journey she took thereafter. Hearing this story, swallowing down the teenage emotions that she felt at that time, gives very real insight into what many women feel who have traveled similar paths. Having had first-hand experience with abortion myself, then spending years of my life speaking at pregnancy care centers to women has shown me time and time again of the need for these kinds of stories to be shared. The narrative of what we now know as commonplace in our society needs to shift. It is through real dialogue from courageous people who are not afraid to share their journey that we can see that shift take place.

Abortion has continued to be a polarizing issue since Roe v. Wade. As a society, I believe we have lost touch with the impact that abortion has on individuals. At a time when a national discussion is taking place, Toni's story could not be better timed. I believe that her journey can help people receive a new understanding for those questioning abortion, and for those who have had one. The emotional impacts of having an abortion are not spoken of often enough. There are many people suffering in silence, or more heartbreakingly, continuing not to see how their abortion negatively impacted their own lives. Toni's story is one that shows clarity through healing. It shows how taking ownership of past mistakes can often bring about the most effective and positive changes within one's own life.

As the founder and president of Urban CURE, the Center for Urban Renewal and Education, I work hard to engage in discussions on how to help transition America's poor from government dependency to self-sufficiency. I founded CURE in 1995 to bring new ideas to policy discussions. Our organization is a think tank with all manner of data at our fingertips. The numbers and statistical data show a long line of destruction where abortion is concerned. People think of the mother who has had the abortion, and rightly so. But many fail to think about the father. Many forget about that teen's parent or friend who may have encouraged the abortion to begin with. Many often forget to think about the baby. The negative emotional impact of having an abortion has very long, long legs. The tragedy of which continues to ripple through the life and lives of those involved. As a society, we need strong voices to help teach others the truth about abortion, about the very real aftereffects of having had one, and about how abortion is a crime against humanity. Just because things are legal does not make them lawful in God's eyes, and that has a crippling effect that ripples over time, causing destruction without and within.

When hearing this story for the first time, all those years ago without nearly as many details as this book holds, I was struck by the fact that Toni's is a true love story. It is the ultimate love story of someone waiting in the shadows for their beloved to notice them. God waited, and with one perfectly timed invitation, Toni answered His call. She came to Him a sinner, as we all are. She came to Him hopeful for a new way. He greeted her, embraced her, and surrounded her within His healing love. He taught her about His love, how to love herself, and ultimately how to love others by using her story.

The road that Toni traveled was not easy; let's face it, most of us have traveled a hard road. At the culmination of our most difficult journeys are often the most beautiful destinations. Toni's road has paved the way for others to be empowered in their choices. She has helped scared mothers turn away from the facilities that seek to take their children. She has helped those who have been broken by abortion to begin their healing. While those of us who have had an abortion know that we can receive healing from and through God, we all know that there is no cure for the deep guilt we will carry with us through the rest of our lives. It is by sharing very real experiences, as Toni has done, that we hope will shift those away from abortion and encourage our entire society to choose life.

I feel very honored to have been asked to write this foreword for such a young, powerful motivator within the pro-life movement. Toni's growth the past few years within the pro-life movement has continued to ignite the hope of all of those fighting for life. I look forward to seeing the continued success for all of those that her story touches.

Serving you,

Star Parker

INTRODUCTION

1-23-99

Dear Diary,

This is the hardest day in my life. Today I found out I was pregnant. I cried so hard. I can't believe this happened to me. I'm waiting for Kris to call now. My best friend is here. She came right over when I told her. She found a place in Allentown that performs abortions. She's going to help me pay for it if I don't have enough.

I just talked to Kris. He's being really sweet. He told me he'd go with me to get the abortion. He's also going to give me money. He said he'd be here for me. This is the sweetest he's ever been. This makes me love him even more. I feel like I can trust him with anything. He's a totally different person. My bestie is going to call for me on Monday. I just want this to be over with. I'm not having sex for a long time. I don't even want to. I feel so dead and trapped.

Kris says I should calm down, that everything's going to be fine. I really hope it is . . .

This is the worst thing that has ever happened to me. I respect him more because like other guys, he wasn't a jerk. I love that he's going to be there for me. Things are hard right now, but I think it will make me stronger. I think this will also bring us closer together. We are always going to be a part of each other's lives now. Every time I look at him, I'm going to think I could have had a girl or boy with him, and he'll think the same. I'll wonder what he or she would have looked like.

I'm going to be a different person. I'm already starting to look at things differently. There's no way I could have a baby now. The hard part will be having the abortion. If my parents ever found out, my life would truly be over. I feel like my life's over now. I just keep thinking there's a little person slowly growing inside of me and because of my stupidity, its life is going to end. It's not fair, but I have no other choice.

I don't think I want to have sex anymore anyway. It's not so special when a tiny life is involved. Kris calls it bad timing. I call it bad judgment on both our parts. God, please look after me. I know you're not proud of me right now, but I really need you . . . Amen, Toni.

It's difficult looking back now and reading that journal entry from all those years ago. It's embarrassing. It's hard to know the details of the journey I would travel because of all the things I believed, mistakenly, in my young mind.

It's my sincere hope that this book will reach the hearts of those who may have traveled down a similar road. I hope you know that you are not alone, and that healing is possible.

I pray that this book will help clear up some confusion for our youth regarding sex and relationships. I pray this book will be for them what I desperately needed at their age. If you are reading this and you are facing an unplanned pregnancy, please know that you can choose life and that there are resources to help you.

I pray that you feel strength and hope as you read through my story. May the words on these pages reveal hope, love, and forgiveness.

—Toni McFadden

CHAPTER 1

The Waiting Room

I wish I could forget the feelings I had while sitting in that place. It's funny because I do not remember walking in, or even driving there. I do remember sitting in the waiting room. It was a room the size of my bedroom. I remember thinking there were so many girls there. Were they all there for the same reason? I looked around at their faces and tried to see if they were feeling like I was. Some looked scared, others nervous, most looked numb. Yes, I thought, we were there for the same reason.

That momentous day at work flashed back in my mind, the cold, mid-January day, when I realized I was late. It was early into my shift at a local pharmacy when I registered this very important detail. My breasts had been sore, but that didn't mean anything special. Ok sure, I had been eating more at lunch. Some girls experienced that with their normal cycles, maybe mine was just evolving. I noticed my chest looked bigger, too. But come on, other girls talked about that, too. Normally, you could set a clock to my cycle. It always came on time. I always had the same symptoms. This was different, "So, am I . . .?"

A customer momentarily interrupted my thoughts, but a few minutes later, I revisited. I tried to shake the feeling, tried to shake the thoughts that were now swirling in my head at a thousand miles a minute. I needed to take a test immediately. Finally, it was time for me to take my lunch break. I grabbed two pregnancy tests on my way to the employee lounge. Straight into the bathroom I went with a cold sweat now breaking out. Hands slightly shaking as I, for the first time ever, administered a pregnancy test to myself.

I'm in high school; I can't be pregnant! This is just to make myself feel better; it's not going to be positive. But it was. They both were, and in that moment, everything that I knew in my life went spiraling into a dark abyss. I needed to return to my shift, but in my head, I was already talking to my best friend about what the heck I was supposed to do now.

The remaining hours of my shift saw me moving on autopilot, the whole time having a large internal debate about how I was going to deal with this. How was I going to tell Kris? What was he going to say? The only reason I had slept with him to begin with was because I didn't want him to slip away. I loved him, for sure. I had not been ready for the step of sleeping together. I knew it would have been a risk if I didn't sleep with him. He could have easily found other girls at college who would. How was I supposed to compete with that? Now look, look at what happened! My mind continued to spin with thoughts spiraling faster than I could process. The result of it all was sheer panic. Finally, my shift ended, and I went to the only person I thought I could talk to.

Sitting across from my best friend, I blurted, "I'm pregnant!"

"You have to get rid of it," was the very first thing out of her mouth. During the next few minutes, she was very much in charge. "I know what to do. We just call the abortion clinic, and we will get it all taken care of." And she did. In just a few minutes, I had handed over the control of this giant situation to her. *Oh, thank goodness, someone knows what to do*, I thought.

The hours seemed to tick by the remainder of that day. My brain continued in overdrive as I tried to swallow the fact that there was a baby inside of me. It was easily the most emotionally terrifying thing I had ever felt so far in my life. I guessed it was good that my best friend knew what to do. She was making the calls to gather information, taking care of things. She even took care of that call to Kris. The one I could not quite seem to get myself to make, the one I was dreading and putting off, the one I could not handle.

"You don't want to keep it, do you?" Kris asked by way of my best friend.

"I guess . . . not," I murmured. Did I mean that? Was that just the fear talking? I never allowed myself the time to think it through. I knew what we were planning to do was wrong. The whole thing was filled with so many levels of wrong, but I did not let myself think over it. I had a life to live. I had a future to figure out. I was in no position to birth a baby. This was the only option; there was nothing else to be done. My best friend, Kris, and I had made this plan. Now, we just had to stick with it. No one else needed to know.

My best friend had tracked down the appropriate place for me to go and had given me the number. Calling to make the appointment had been an interesting experience. After the details were taken by the kind woman on the other end of the phone, a date was set. Before we hung up, the same kind lady said, "Now when we call back to confirm your appointment, we will be using a different name. That name is our code word to you, so you will know it's us and know what it is regarding, but your parents will not." *Wow*, I thought. This was so incredibly kind of them. They are keeping my secret, working with me.

I tried to think of another time or situation where another adult would have helped me keep such a big secret from my parents, especially a medical-related secret. I came up short and felt intense relief that these people were on my side. Six days, I had to wait six whole days before my appointment.

A few days later, I stood in front of the refrigerator, looking for a snack. I could hear the chatter of my family in the living room. I wish I could tell them what was going on, but I knew it would disappoint them. All the usual things were going on, the usual conversations, the usual sounds, and voices. I looked down at my stomach, again realizing that there was something growing inside me. It hit me then that their lives were unchanged by this gigantic event happening right before them. All their lives continued as they always had, completely untouched. Here I was, and it felt like the walls in my young life were crashing all around me. Everything I had worked for was teetering on the verge of collapsing.

It was strange to realize that as I stood in that moment with them, the realities were incredibly different. They were on one side, and I was on the much darker, other side: My parents were thinking that their good little girl was about to graduate high school with a wonderful future ahead of her. They would be in shock to find out my choices had led me on a path that "troubled" teens have found themselves in. I couldn't help but think of the fact that I was pregnant and needed not to be.

They were probably thinking I would never do anything to screw my future up. I knew I just had. I felt frozen and panicked to the point that my best friend had to step in and do the plans.

I wanted to shout, "There is a *MAJOR* life event happening right now." But I held silent, shut the refrigerator, and walked quietly to my bedroom, closing the door between our realities.

From that point forward, I played a polite, balancing act with myself. I juggled between the reality around me and the real one inside of me. My appointment seemed a lifetime away. I was keeping a secret. I was deceiving the people I loved. This felt like the opposite of who I was, but it would be ok soon. Soon, it would all be over, and my life would continue like it had been. Everything was going to be just fine, right? It seemed as though I asked myself this question every hour over those days.

Knowing that Kris was going to come with me made me feel lucky. I felt a weird sense of support at the time, though looking back on it I am not so sure that was his motivation. At the moment, I thought we were really in it together. He loved me enough to be a part of this with me. Relief washed over me in those moments when I thought about his support. He was with me, which made me feel very fortunate.

Finally, it was time. My best friend, Kris, and I loaded into her car to make the evening drive to my appointment. The sun was setting as we drove, and I couldn't help but draw a morbid connection to this moment in my own life. I knew what we were going to do; I had made that decision already. All I wanted was for my life to go back to normal without anybody finding out I had gotten pregnant. Now I was on autopilot, a disconnected robot moving myself toward the only thing I thought reasonable to do at this time.

I walked into the back of the building on shaky legs. My best friend sat by my side, and Kris sat across from me. I was shaking so badly Kris kept reaching over to try to calm my legs down. Or maybe he just wanted to touch me, to offer comfort. No, Kris never showed affection in public. He was just trying to get me to calm down. I looked around and saw all those other girls sitting there with blank expressions on their faces. We were all numb, I realized. All of us were just pushing through it to do what we thought had to be done.

The abortion facility felt empty, devoid of any sort of comforting or happy emotions. There was a stale stench in the air mingled with cleaning products. I realized there was no life here. It was as if the spirit of death had come to live in this place. I'd never felt so inherently cold, sad, or numb when visiting a doctor before. I did not let myself settle into these thoughts, though.

"Toni Davis," I heard the nurse call through my foggy contemplation. I stood and began walking toward her. Halfway to the doorway, I registered that Kris had not moved. My heart sank to the floor. He had not gotten up to come with me. I looked back at him; I wanted to see something there. I wanted to see his support, the love he professed to have. I wanted to see some remnant of the relationship we had spent time investing in. He did not move. He did not even look up at me as I stood staring longingly into the side of his face. Up to this moment, I had thought we were in this together. He did not look at me though, just sat there, looking anywhere else but at me.

With my best friend at my side, and seven-week-old- baby growing inside me, I faced forward and walked ahead. The ultrasound was first, and as I lay on the table, I remember thinking it was odd that the monitor was facing the wall. I would later learn that the monitor had been strategically placed, facing away from anyone who lay upon that table. I asked the nurse to turn it so I could see the screen. Both my best friend and the nurse agreed that it would be better for me if I did not look. I insisted. I did not know why seeing the baby was so important to me; it just was. "See," the nurse replied frustrated, "it's nothing. It's just the size of a pea." I searched the monitor, looking for something that resembled a baby. I saw a shadowed circle. That was it. Nothing.

In my scared teenage mind, hearing that made me feel better. *It's not a baby yet; it's nothing. I am doing this early enough*, I thought, *before it's a real baby. I'm not like all those other girls who do this to an actual baby. It's not a baby yet; it's nothing.*

They brought me back to the waiting room. The gray coldness seemed even heavier now as I waited for the next part. I kept looking at Kris, wondering what he was thinking. I would catch him staring at me a lot, but he would look away quickly. I felt reassured again that in his way, he was trying to comfort me. His immobility just a few minutes ago was forgotten as I clung to the only thing inside the room that made me feel warm, my love for him.

I got called back inside so that a nurse could explain, briefly, what was going to happen when I took the pills, they were going to give me. Then I was hustled into that awful waiting room, again. I kept wondering where that nice lady who had taken my initial phone call was. Her voice sounded so kind, so comforting. I wished she was with me now, speaking her kindness into me. It would have eased my nerves, would have calmed my soul. Instead, anxiety shot through me.

The last time they called my name, it was time to see the doctor. The fear jacked up higher as I was told to undress from the waist down so the doctor could examine me. *A pelvic exam? I don't even know what that is*, I thought as I was left to strip down. The male doctor walked in shortly. He had an air of boredom about him. He vaguely explained what he was going to do for my examination. For my first time having an exam like this, it was pretty much the most uncomfortable thing I had experienced in a doctor's office to date. I still was not quite sure what he was doing, or why he needed to be doing it. I did not understand why he just expected me to know what I was supposed to be doing. He seemed impervious to my confusion, completely detached from the fact that I was afraid. I was just some teen who had gotten pregnant, just another among many.

Still, I trusted him. My entire life I had always gone to a doctor when something was wrong, and they fixed it. They made it better; that's what doctors did. I ignored my feelings of discomfort. I never thought to ask any questions as he handed me a cup of red juice into which he dropped two pills. RU-486 pills also called Mifepristone. I did not realize it then, but the purpose of these abortion pills was to block the hormone progesterone. As a result, my baby would detach from my uterus, starve, and die because the baby would no longer receive nourishment or blood flow from me.[1] At the time, I was not concerned with what he gave me; he had my trust merely because he was a doctor. "This will stop the pregnancy." His sentence was short, and very matter of fact.

I swallowed the juice. It is important that I take a moment to recognize that it is possible to reverse the effects of the first set of pills. Progesterone can be given by injection or in the form of a pill. This could possibly save the life of the baby.

He then gave me two additional sets of pills that I would take within a few days, called Misoprostol.[2] It never occurred to me to ask him what he had given me or the details of what would happen when I took them. I never asked about side effects; who thinks of those things as a teenager? He explained I would at some point in the next few days bleed a little heavier than a normal period. He made it sound like it would be brief and over quickly. I felt relieved; this doctor was making everything better. I wouldn't have to hide this secret any longer; it was over. I won't be pregnant anymore. I don't have to face my parents over this. I can breathe again.

As I walked back to the car, the momentary relief I felt was gone. A deep, ugly sense of dread was seeping up. I was helpless to stop it. I kept

---

1   "Abortion Pill Reversal," Abortion Pill Rescue Network, 12/26/21, https://abortionpill-reversal.com/the-abortion-pill
2   Abortion Pill Rescue Network, 2021.

thinking; *I can't believe I did this.* The ride home was long. I was lying in the backseat, feeling completely alone. The sounds of Kris and my best friend talking as if nothing life-changing had just taken place only made me feel worse. How were they ok right now? Tears streamed down my face as my body warred between relief and guilt. I made up my mind not to go back to that horrible place. No one prepared me for this. No one told me I would feel this way. They made it sound so easy. No nurse, or even the doctor, prepared me for this unexpected crying or these dreadful feelings that were inside me.

My best friend drove me home first. I had to push through my emotions and the feeling of being foggy as I got out of the car. Kris got out as well, gave me a hug and a kiss on the cheek. I registered the touch and was surprised by it. He said he would call me tomorrow; I hoped he would. I went inside with the substantial weight of my emotions still threatening to drown me. I made it through that night with all the foulness festering within, though I could not tell you how I passed the time.

The next day I called Kris. He did not answer.

I resolved later that morning, with puffy eyes, to put my energy into a new focus, not letting my family find out what I had done. I still had the additional pills to take and knew that my best friend's house was the logical place for me to take them. I made the arrangements and a night later, saw us sitting together in her room like we had a hundred times before, so no suspicion from my family there. I took the first set of pills, which caused me to bleed a tiny bit after a few hours. I called the clinic the next morning because I had been told I would bleed heavier than a normal period, and I had barely had any blood. Their tone was completely different from when I had first called. Where was the kindness? In an indifferent and unsympathetic tone, they simply said, "Take the second set of pills, you should be fine. A little cramping and bleeding and that is all." I took the second set of pills later that night per their instructions. Again, I had just a little spotting. I was not that far along. I imagined that this spotting was exactly what was supposed to happen; after all, it wasn't quite a baby yet; it was "nothing," right?

I had tried calling Kris a few times by this point and had gotten no answer. I knew this was deliberate. After a few unanswered calls, and his lack of checking in, I realized he was closing the door on our relationship. My heart was broken. The grief I had not expected from aborting my unborn baby was choking me already. Now, I had to come to terms with the fact that my on again/off again boyfriend of two years had just abandoned me to my pain and caused me more. He had walked out of my life with finality, slamming the door on anything we had together. Leaving my calls unanswered was the loudest way he could have expressed his feelings. I knew I had to move on. I had to get up and go to school. I had to pretend like nothing earth-shattering had just happened. Graduation was on the horizon, and I needed to focus forward.

The things around me continued at a normal pace, and it got easier to push my thoughts and feelings behind me. The days of forcing a numb smile to my face unconsciously started to give way. Slowly, I began to feel happiness again. I sat in music class one day, a month or so later, surrounded by all the usual faces. I loved music class; singing always made me happy.

Surrounded by my friends, I prepared to warm up, as I did in every class. Out of nowhere, I started to feel sharp, shooting pains running through my entire body. *Am I due for my period?* As I thought about it, the cramping got worse. Faster than I could register, my body began to shake from the intense pain. What was going on? Within a few minutes, I knew I was in trouble. Thankfully, a friend offered to assist me to the nurse's office.

I was an almost deadweight on her as she helped me make the journey to the nurse's office. The pain was loudly thumping through my body. Every step I took shook up through me and caused the cramping to intensify. As soon as I reached the office, I went straight to the restroom. What I saw coming out of me was horrifying! Blood clots the size of my fist were leaving my body.

Through the fear and intense pain, it dawned on me that the pills from all those many months ago had not worked completely. I was now, months later, passing out the baby I had tried so hard to get rid of. The pain continued to roll through me as I tried to make sense of what was happening, knowing the entire time that I couldn't tell the nurse the truth. I convinced the nurse that this was just a particularly intense time of the month, not an unusual occurrence for me.

My mom came to pick me up, believing the lie I had successfully sold the nurse. When we got home, I went straight to the bathroom. More blood clots left my body. The pain churned within me for hours. I lay on my bed in between the trips to the bathroom, horrified at what I was seeing in the toilet, trying to erase the images from my mind. Curled on my side in an ironic fetal position, I prayed for this to be over soon. My brain would try to ask questions to clarify what I was feeling, seeing. I kept telling myself, *we can't go there. Don't think about it.* Fear and confusion were swooshing in from all sides, mixing with the pain to form some sort of nightmarish cocktail. For some reason, maybe by God's grace, I cannot remember past this point of that dreadful day.

CHAPTER 2

It's All a Party!

Life resumed after that. I was getting good at going through the motions. I had never understood that phrase until this year. I guess you do grow a lot during senior year, though a part of me doubted that this was the type of growth one should aspire to achieve. Again, I was numb until one day the happiness began to seep in, and I could feel the laughter again. Graduation day finally arrived. I was sure it was all behind me now. The day was moving quickly with my class gathering for the ceremony. The sound of laughter and happy tears swirled around me in a symphony of energy. I was swept up in it until I wasn't.

Of course, this would be the day that I found out that Kris was dating another girl from my class. *What? There aren't girls in college for you to date? You have to come back to high school and date someone right in my face? How could you make the effort to date her when you just walked away from me without a word on the very day I had to abort our baby?* The anger and hurt mixed and threatened the happiness the day had held. I just wanted this to be behind me.

I squared my shoulders against the onslaught of emotions. I was so mad that this saga was touching the happiness I should feel on this day. I made it to graduation. I made it without my parents finding out what I had done. I made it with my reputation of "good girl" intact for them, and for myself. I was determined to move on with my life. *If I could just get away from the memories of it all*, I thought, *then things would be normal again.*

I was staying local for college and sort of stumbled into my new phase of life. I began college with what I imagine is the same nervous, excited energy that most college freshmen feel. The new sense of independence felt like the first time you open the door in spring and smell the freshly cut grass. I was stepping forward, or was I?

I fell in sync at college with what many of the other kids seemed to be doing. I joined a sorority. I went to parties. I drank. I dated. I pursued men single-mindedly. Life moved from one day to the next, with me drowning out the noise of my past the best way I knew how. I continued down this road of partying, of being a barely acceptable student for a little over a year.

I found myself bouncing from one guy to the next. It felt good in the moment. I felt alive, exhilarated. Was there any substance to these encounters? I convinced myself there was. Intimacy was the first step to finding someone to love me, right? I craved being loved by someone. The attention I received from guys somehow validated me. If I wanted to feel beautiful, attention from a guy would do that. I floated like this for months, stomping the same path, hitting the same parties, flowing with the same circles. Something in me wanted more than how I was living my life. I wasn't sure what it looked like.

One day out of the blue, my thoughts shifted. I realized that I could not stay in this place, in my hometown, anymore. When I looked around,

I saw everyone just doing the same thing. My part in it all seemed boring to me suddenly, and sort of sad, though I was not sure why. Staying here just felt like the wrong path. I started thinking about what I was good at, what did I have a talent for? I could sing. I could sing well. It made me happy to sing and perform. Where performing often caused anxiety for some, I thrived in it. It was naturally a part of who I was. I began looking into colleges that were close enough to my family but far enough away for a change. My search brought me to West Chester University. I navigated the application process with no help from my parents or school advisor. It was the first major life decision I was undertaking completely by myself. I impressed myself with how I was able to get this done.

When it came time to audition, I was nervous but excited. I was looking forward to taking the stage and feeling the joy of it wash over me. When I sang, there was safety, security, and strength. Singing was the one area of my life where I had always been fully confident in my abilities. I knew I would do well that day. I knew, too, that this was a step. I wasn't sure what I was stepping toward, but I knew I was stepping outside of my comfort zone. It felt good.

I was thrilled when I received my acceptance to West Chester University. The pride I felt in myself for figuring things out was a brand-new feeling for me. I immediately began working out the financial details, another significant "adult thing" I had done so far in my journey. The excitement of taking this step overshadowed the smaller steps I had taken with college previously. The feeling that I was on the cusp of a real adventure blossomed inside of me. I felt genuine hopefulness for whatever lay ahead. Things were going to be different!

Summer was nearly here, and my hometown was alive with the buzz of vacationers and summer crowds. I was in my last semester at East Stroudsburg University, still spending my days as I had since the beginning. The parties beefed up at school. It was at one such party that

I met and began to date a very nice rugby player. He was a little older than me with an appreciation for me that I did not yet understand. It was the first genuine relationship I had ever had. I was in over my head, though I did not know it.

I was living with some friends at an apartment off-campus and working as a waitress at a local chain restaurant. The money was decent, and the hours worked well with school. I still managed to have quite a social life while navigating school and work. I always had time for a party and seeing my new boyfriend.

While working one day, I ran into a familiar face from high school. We had never been what I would call friends, but we knew one another's faces well enough to be friendly. Upon catching up briefly, we both discovered that we were off to West Chester University come the fall semester. We decided to be roommates in that very brief conversation. While I was excited to go off to a place where I knew no one, it would still be nice to see a familiar face. Who knew, maybe we'd be the best of friends by the end of it?

At night, I would often head to my boyfriend's place to sleep. There was more privacy at his place than at mine. I loved the moments we had together. We shared silly moments, drunken stories, laughter, music, and all-around fun. I pursued him, made myself readily available for and to him. As the summer drew to a close, there was an ever-present knot in my stomach at the thought of leaving him.

We talked about how we would handle the distance. I had to push back the memories of Kris when he went off to college. I had to remind myself that just because I often felt like a distant memory to Kris when he was away at college did not mean that it would feel the same this time. We were a different couple. It would be ok. He seemed very much at peace with our long-distance arrangement. I had to leave him, I reminded myself. I did not want to hold myself back. I wanted this new adventure; I knew that I did. Still, there were moments where I was sure that I wanted him more.

The day was finally upon me. My mom and Dad dropped me off at my new school. Reality started settling in. Was this really happening? I've never lived far from my parents before. I had so much nervous energy buzzing around me. I could tell this was difficult for my mom. I was really doing this and making a path for myself.

The sea of swarming new faces made me feel giddy and nervous, all at once. New people, new friends, new experiences. It was happening! I could not believe I had done this. I had figured this all out on my own, and today was the day it would all start. I stepped forward toward my future.

"The heart of man plans his way, but the Lord establishes his steps." -Proverbs 16:9 (English Standard Version)

The excitement and determination I felt during my arrival at West Chester University faded fast. I should have been focused on all the things I wanted—new friends, new experiences. My determination for a new start was long forgotten in a few short days. Instead, I was focused on driving back to my hometown to see my boyfriend. It had been hard to leave him. We had discussed how we would manage the distance; it seemed like it would be ok. I was hoping we could make it work. No, I was committed to making it work! Had I met him before I had begun my journey to change schools, I would never have taken this step. He was the kind of man worth sticking around for. God's hand was again at work, unbeknownst to me, for my life would have been largely altered had I not made this move, had I stayed there for him.

I spent most of the first month driving back to East Stroudsburg to be with my boyfriend. I was so invested in my relationship that I had forgotten what this change was for. My single-minded focus sharpened more intensely on him from a distance. I got nervous if I could not get in touch with him. I felt fear that I would lose him to someone who was in school with him. I knew he wasn't fickle, but my own insecurities "reared their ugly faces," ferociously from the distance. The fear within me only heightened my desire to be with him more. I came back to what I always did, move forward, and pursue, focus on my target, and draw all my energy into it.

When September 11, 2001, hit, things took a turn in our relationship. Our nation was in shock. I remember everyone feeling so helpless. My boyfriend was a former serviceman, he had concerns that I was too immature to truly understand. He began to talk about things that were much deeper than I could truly swallow at this time. I had not grown enough, yet. I could sense that his ambitions for his future were more advanced than I could comprehend, and it became clear that we were not on the same page. I did not want to admit it, but I could sense him slipping away. All my fears were coming to the surface once again. I was trying to make things work, while he was pulling away. We broke up at the beginning of October. I did not take this well, even though I had realized we were not in the same place. I had wanted someone to love me. He loved me in his own way. Not perfectly but better than the other boyfriend's that I had. I rejoined the party crowd, immersing myself in every bad college habit I had previously engaged in. Nothing was different; I was just in a different place, doing the same old thing. A few weeks later, on a Thirsty Thursday, I walked into the local bar we affectionately called "The Rat." I felt sick at the smell of beer, sick of the fake intimacy found after a long night of drinking, sick of myself. But hey, it was college; this is what you did, right? I tipped the beer back and shoved my thoughts down.

CHAPTER 3

Growing in Faith

"What comes into our minds when we think about God is the most important thing about us."—A. W. Tozer

A few weeks later, a friend from my hometown who happened to live on the same dorm and floor as me, invited me to go to a Campus Crusade meeting with her. I knew this was a Christian ministry. I had heard of it and was vaguely aware of the fact that they got together weekly. It was Thursday; was I going to go to this meeting instead of the bar? I heard myself tell her I would go. She had chosen her moment to ask me well. I was tired of the party scene even though I had done nothing to change it for myself. It was where most people were, where I could socialize. It was a distraction. I was broken-hearted and desperately searching for a place to help me forget my pain. This was something new, a new experience with new people. Maybe I could forget all the heartache for just a little while tonight.

Before this night, I would have said I was a Christian. I believed God was real. I believed He had died on the cross for my sins. That was the foundation of my beliefs. I went to church sporadically with my family. I tried to be a good person. I would soon find out that there was so much more to saying, "I am a Christian," then I realized.

No stranger to entering an auditorium, having been a singer for more years than I could count at this point, I felt confident entering. We walked through the auditorium doors. My eyes adjusted to the low lights in the room while the stage pulled focus with its brightly illuminated presence. Music filled the air, and I heard, "Come, now is the time to worship. Come, now is the time to give your heart. Come, just as you are to worship. Come, just as you are before your God." The hairs on my arms prickled.

I moved forward. As I walked slowly down the aisle, I let the music fill me. I looked around at the students. Hands were raised, eyes were closed, smiles were bright. Everyone seemed peaceful, calm, and happy. I noticed there were probably close to two hundred students in the auditorium on a Thursday night when most college kids were out drinking. They had chosen to be here. That thought hit me like a ton of bricks. I was missing something.

About halfway down the aisle, I sat down, devouring the sights around me. The music continued to swell. Students stood together, singing joyously. I took everything in, letting it wash over me. That was the first time that night that tears began to fill my eyes. I took some deep, steadying breaths. Why did I feel like crying?

As the night progressed, different leaders stood to speak and share. Their messages slammed into me one after another. I felt as though I had been in a desert for years, my body so thirsty for water that it was soaking in these words through every pore. Again, tears threatened to emerge, and again, I squashed them down. Speakers continued to share, and the music continued to circulate the air in an overwhelmingly powerful way. I cannot say how many times I fought back my tears that night.

At one point during the announcements, the leader said that there were a few of the worship leaders who were graduating in December. He added that they would be holding auditions for worship singers shortly. I had felt inspired listening to the worship leaders that night. Wouldn't that be an amazing thing to do? I knew that my life was in no way a testament to Christian leadership. In the back of my mind, though, I knew it would be such an awesome thing to be a part of. Maybe someday.

The worship team was taking a break, so we were all free to mingle around the auditorium. I sat comfortably in my seat, taking it all in when a tiny, little, red-haired girl with this big, curly hair came over and welcomed me. "Hi, my name is Katie!" Katie had seen me around and announced that she did a Bible Study in our dorm. She was an incredibly vibrant person. I was in awe over how she could confidently just come up to me and be so open. She offered to stop by one day, so we could go to lunch. I agreed and continued my admiration of her as she confidently moved from person to person around the room. She was so full of life, and it seemed like being that welcoming came naturally to her. She was one of few different people who stood out to me that night. I liked how I felt here, in this room, with these people on a Thursday night that usually consisted of me drinking.

I managed to hold myself together until I got back to my room. The overwhelming urge to cry had continued to rise despite my best efforts to squelch it. I held it in though. I held back. I could not break down in front of these strangers. They were all walking around so joyfully. They would not understand what I was feeling.

I shut my dorm room door behind me, lay down on my bed, and cried. There was nothing gentle about this outpouring. It came on fast and strong. It was a bottomless sobbing, a strenuous and exhausting cry that came from so deep inside of me. I was desperate for God to change me. I wanted to feel the peace, the joy, and the happiness that all of those inside that auditorium were feeling. I wanted to be able to get up on that stage and lead worship, not because I loved to sing, but because I wanted to make others feel as I had felt tonight. It was inspiring. It was hopeful. How long had it been since I had been inspired by something so purely wholesome? How long had it been since I had felt hopeful? I couldn't recall.

I knew my life was in a rut and had felt it for some time. I had thought the move to a new school would somehow align things, but things still felt empty. Life was somehow spiraling. I had no idea where to start or what direction to look in to affect change. I did not like who I was. Through my tears I offered up a child-like prayer and asked Jesus to help me. God heard my unspoken prayers. It was that night I believe Jesus saved my soul.

Katie, with the curly red hair, showed up at my door within days. Her effervescent aura was like the shining sun in my confusing world. She gently helped me close the gap between knowing I needed a change and teaching me a way forward in that change. She introduced me to Bible Study. I began getting up every morning at 6 a.m. to start my day reading the Bible, devouring each word. God's grace was all over every moment of my days from that point forward.

I cultivated new friendships with people who were not in the party scene. Instead, they spent time at Bible Study, or within the community in different service opportunities. They studied hard and tried to use their skills to serve those around them. This was an entirely new way of thinking for me. I watched, eyes glued, to learn new skills that I could use myself. My daily readings paved the way to Sunday services. I continued to be introduced to other people who were making their way in life with the Lord, and I was in awe.

A month later, I tried out for the worship team with Campus Crusade. I could feel the transformation God had led in my life, and I was eager to share it with others. I would wake up excited daily now. The fun I had was wholesome, and there was a calming effect on my life. It was a new feeling for me. I tried and failed to put it into words often. I knew though that I was somehow surrounded by a very special sort of blanket, and I was eager to stay cozy within it. It wasn't that every day was perfect; it was more that my life finally had a sense of purpose.

The holidays came upon me fast that year. I listened to many of my peers recount their first visits home after becoming a Christian. I knew that they had all felt tested during those visits. I was nervous to go home. I was nervous I would be around too many things that were familiar from my old life, and I did not yet feel strong enough to do this without the ever-present support I had at college. I knew what my friends back home had been doing. Katie and my other new friends had warned me of what to expect. I took their warning the way most people would have taken it, with a grain of salt, convinced that my convictions were all I needed to get me through. I was excited to see my family. I was so on fire with my commitment to being a Christian, I was looking forward to sharing it with them. I made my drive back to East Stroudsburg, PA.

It was during that visit home that I learned about and truly felt the grief of the Holy Spirit. As my friends gathered to go from one party to the next, I watched with mixed feelings. I wanted to be with my friends, to partake in their fun. Yet, I knew that partaking in that way would only lead me back to the bad habits that I was not eager to repeat. I felt remorse for my partying in a way I never had before. It rocked me with a sadness I had not expected. It showed me clearly that the enemy was always at work and that I needed the strong support of those around me to help stay the course. Sadly, those support systems were not in place here in my hometown the way they were on my college campus. For now, until I was stronger, I was going to have to remember that when I came home.

With that lesson learned over the Thanksgiving break, I was eager to not repeat the same mistakes during Christmas. I signed up for a Christmas Conference to attend. I figured giving myself another way to grow closer to God would help me grow stronger. I was right. There was a vendor area that we were able to walk around. It was during some downtime that I came across a table for Keynote Music Ministry that was based out in Indianapolis, which was run by Campus Crusade. They had an upcoming mission trip in which a worship band would be able to travel around to different churches to lead worship for their respective congregations. I had experienced real growth within myself in just the few days I had attended this conference and felt inspired to do more. I decided I was going to audition for the Keynote Missions trip that would be happening the following summer. This was not an easy process, but thankfully my friends from Campus Crusade were eager to help. They helped me create the audition video that I would be sending in as well as fill out my testimony. People from all over the United States were applying for the opportunity to attend this mission trip. Through God's hand, I was chosen.

I worked diligently to improve as a student during this time. My new commitment to my faith spurred a desire to do my best in every aspect of my life. I started to take my college experience seriously for the first time, eagerly devouring information in my educational course of study as well as my faith. My commitment to Campus Crusade every Thursday night did not waver. Reading the Bible each day continued to show me that I was at once gaining in my relationship with God while simultaneously revealing that I still had a long way to go. Some days the verses were easy to understand, others I had to work harder, and even others I would not understand the verses for years to come. I was busy, but there was balance and a beginning of the peace that I had longed for.

I had to work hard over those months and added to that work was my fundraising efforts for my mission trip. If I was going to go on this trip, I needed to cover my cost. I did not know the first thing about fundraising for something like this. I was completely out of my element. I knew that if that was where God wanted me, He would provide all that I needed. That is exactly what He did! It was moments like this that grew my faith. And just like that, I was going on my first mission trip. I could not believe it. I was blown away by the generosity of those who gave to my mission trip. This was the community I was surrounded by, and it amazed me.

It was one of those wonderful, slow afternoons. My schoolwork was complete, and I had nowhere to be. I lay on my couch with my Bible in my lap, thinking about the fast-approaching summer of 2002. Before I knew it, the spring semester would be over, and I would be off on my trip. *Where would I live come fall semester*, I wondered? Despite my best efforts to secure a place and roommates, I was still without. It had been on my mind a lot recently, as it seemed everyone already had this squared away. What would I do if I did not find a place to live? I belonged here within this community. It was the exact right fit for all the things I needed to learn at that time. I could not imagine what would happen if I was somehow not able to come back in the fall. I flipped open the Bible and landed on Joshua 1:9, *"Have I not commanded you? Be strong and coura- geous. Do not be frightened, and do not be dismayed, for the Lord your God is with you wherever you go."* Wow, what a powerful verse! I mulled it over for a while before the afternoon heat whisked me off into a nap.

Before too long, I was in the throes of a nightmare. Everything was dark; my chest was so heavy. Unseen demons were on my neck, choking me. I couldn't breathe. My body entered a full panic mode as I fought off the invisible demons for my life. I screamed out, "Jesus!" A hand appeared from above and reached for me. All at once, the darkness turned to light, the heaviness gave way, and I was pulled up to reality from the depths of darkness. As I shook off the blanket of the scary sleep I had been in, I realized something was trying to squelch my voice. It was the first time of what would be many that the demons came to visit me in my dreams. I realized that something did not want me on the journey I was on, something wanted me silenced. I wasn't sure why I knew this, but I was certain of it. *Strange*, I thought. I did not have much to say; why would I need to be silent?

A few days later, with Joshua 1:9 fresh in my mind, I departed for my mission's trip to Indianapolis as a part of Keynote Music Ministry to be on the worship team. I had never been on a plane before. I was terrified. I could not turn back now.

On this trip, I grew even more in my faith. I learned what it meant to lead worship in spirit and in truth. Little did I know, God would bless me with an amazing new friendship. Monica entered my life not only as my roommate, but she was on the worship team with me. Monica was a singer, like me. She also, like me, had a desire to strengthen her relationship with God. We eased into a fast friendship, one that would span the test of distance, time, and life's adventures. I had no idea then that I was meeting someone with whom I would develop one of the longest and deepest friendships of my life. We have become so close that we call one another soul Sista's! In the short amount of time on this mission trip, God knitted our hearts together for a purpose.

As young Christians, we were equally excited to gain the fullest experience possible. To be able to lead others into worship, to help them enter the presence of God was incredible.

For so many years, I had been a singer in high school musicals, chorus, choir, at special events. Countless times I had stood before people, both large and small crowds, and I had performed. I loved singing. I felt amazing when I delivered a strong performance. Singing reminded me that I was good at something that could make people feel emotions. It was exhilarating. I had done this for years, allowing those emotions to fill me when I sang. It never occurred to me to thank God for the gift of my voice. Previously, God had not been a factor in my talent at all. It was not until I went to Campus Crusade all those nights ago that I discovered I could use the gift God gave me to help bring people closer to Him. On that first Thursday, I had hoped to lead people in worship. At Campus Crusade, I had earned a place on the worship team. Now, here I was as a worship team member, touring multiple churches to help inspire worship in others. My talent for singing no longer existed to make me feel good; it existed to bring glory to God. Yes, I felt good while doing it, but that was the by-product, not the foundation of my talent. God had shifted this perspective in my life, and once again, I was in awe of the progression my life was taking.

My daily prayer to God the entire time I was away was a plight to help find me a place to live come fall. I knew if I did not find a place, I would have to go back home. That was my worst fear at the time. I knew I was not strong enough to keep up with these changes in my life without the support I was building in college. I had done everything I could think of to do on campus to try to find a place. If something did not turn up, I was facing the worst possible scenario. I was deeply afraid of what that scenario would mean for my newfound faith. It wasn't that I lacked my commitment, more like I knew I needed the support. The changes were all so fresh and new. Changing habits, especially surrounded by the things that triggered bad habits, was nearly impossible. At least I thought so. I hadn't managed to do it in the past. I felt uncertain that I was strong enough to accomplish it if indeed that was to be my future.

It was the day before I was due to fly back home from the mission trip when I called my mom to confirm the flight details. I asked eagerly if anyone had called the house regarding an apartment, and sadly she said no. With only hours left on my mission' trip, I realized that maybe staying at West Chester University was not what God wanted for me. I changed my prayer that day, "God, if you want me to move back home, if that is what will glorify You more, then I will do it." I prayed without disappointment. I prayed honestly and with complete conviction that I would do whatever it was He wanted me to do. On the ride from the airport back to my house, I told my mom that I was willing to accept whatever God wanted for my life. When I entered the house, my dad greeted me and said, "Some girl from Japan called about an apartment."

The shock I felt was mimicked on my mom's face. I excitedly got the details and returned the call. She was in Japan back home with her family and was looking for a roommate to share her apartment with. It would end up being three of us in a small, two-bedroom apartment. The rent was right in my price range. This had God's hand all over it. I accepted the space and was able to return to West Chester University for the fall semester. My faith had reached a new level, and I was eager to see where God wanted me next. Unlike before, I now knew that my prayer to God needed to be different. I needed to always pray for His path, not my own.

"Trust in the Lord with all your heart and lean not on your own understanding; in all your ways acknowledge Him and He will make straight your paths."—Proverbs 3:5-6

CHAPTER 4

The Secret

College life continued to evolve for me. My focus now consisted of singing to the Lord, developing genuine friendships, and learning about God. Alcohol and meaningless intimate moments had no place in my space. It had not been an easy transition, and temptations still haunted me often. I knew this would be the case for the rest of my life. Temptation is and always will be present. The stronger my faith grew, the more I noticed this. I had a solid support system now, though. The friendships I was developing continued to be rooted together in our faith in God, and our individual commitment to living as a Christian to glorify Him. Nothing about this road was easier than any other journey one sets upon. It was simply different and filled with a greater calling than I had ever experienced before.

Campus Crusade became the environment in which I began to realize that God blesses us with gifts. Besides singing, I was not sure I possessed any other gifts, or if I did, they had not yet revealed themselves. It was this line of thought that had me thinking about my performing major. Was that all there was? Was that all I was supposed to do? The natural progression of overthinking for hours led me to think about communications. I guess that sort of went hand in hand with performing, didn't it? Off to the course advisor I went to add a minor to my course of study. After discussion, I realized I had to take a test to add this minor, and I let that thought deter me for about a second. *God does not say the road is easy,* I heard in my head. I jumped in, took the test, passed it, and prepared to learn.

Having added communications as a minor, I had a new appreciation for school. I was no longer just relying on my natural talent for performance. Now, I must cultivate new skills. Filled with what I knew could only be the Holy Spirit, I began to use my public speaking opportunities in class to discuss my newfound faith. In one particular class, surrounded by a large majority of athletes who were well-established leaders of the typical partying community on campus, I spoke about my commitment to waiting for marriage before I had sex again.

Even now, so many years later, I can see their faces. Not one person seemed bored with my talk. Not one person looked away. They were intently watching me, hanging on to my words as I spoke. At that moment, I knew God had revealed another gift He had given me. I was good at speaking. I never would have believed it myself, especially being a newbie to public speaking. I never would have imagined that I could hold the interest of an audience, especially one filled with people who were not beholden to a college experience where abstinence was a priority. After class, one gentleman approached me. He expressed his support of my determination and his respect for my decision, though he had no intention of following suit. He clearly could bridge that difference and see the value in what I had spoken about. A very powerful testament for my first public speech. I was getting the impression that this was just the beginning.

Throughout the next months, I received constant support for not only my communication skills, but for the messages I chose to speak on. Professors and students alike told me it was inspirational to listen to me. This massive encouragement affirmed for me constantly that I was following God's path for my life. In moments of quiet, I marveled at it. I could not believe how drastically different my life continued to be, how amazingly blessed I felt even when things did not work out the way I thought. Especially at those times. I saw God's hand in everything all around me, and I knew I had stumbled on something that would shape the rest of my life though I had no real idea how.

"Every single one of us in this room has a disease, it's called sin. But here is the cure . . ."—Toni McFadden

I was a bulldozer in my commitment to my newfound faith. Jesus saved my soul, and I believed everyone needed to get on board with this. The noise that oftentimes stops people from doing the things they set about did not seem to bother me. I just kept moving forward. If people laughed, I did not notice. I was so on fire for the Lord, I would not be shaken. Visiting home sometimes proved difficult. My family was always loving and supportive, though some were skeptical of the changes within me. They noticed I was not going to the bar, and I was no longer drinking. Some of my family thought this was a phase. Some resented the passion with which I proclaimed that they were not, in fact, the Christians they claimed to be. I cannot imagine this was an easy transition for my family. It was not particularly easy for me either, but at the heart of my family, there has always been love. And love was what got us all through the transitions and growth we all did as individuals.

There was only one subject I never spoke about, the one secret I felt sure I had to keep. That was my abortion. I squashed it down, convinced myself that if I just kept growing in my faith, somehow that incident would be wiped from view. The only people who knew about it certainly were not talking about it, at least not in my circle. I was safe from the smear it could cause in my life now. If I never spoke about it, it was over. I knew. God knew. We could keep it at that. I could continue to move past it, choke it down when the guilt seemed overwhelming. If I kept it quiet, I could keep moving on with my life.

Earlier in the previous year, I had attended Sunday service. It was Sanctity of Human Life Sunday. I had not realized it was this day when I arrived. Greeting those that I knew as I went to sit in the middle of a row, just like I did on every other Sunday. The pastor began to recount how many babies were aborted each year. I looked up in a panic, realizing that there was no way for me to escape without causing a scene. I tried to listen intently, becoming more uncomfortable by the minute. My body temperature was rising, sweat began to pop up all over my body. The pastor continued to talk, though I lost track of his words. I was positive all eyes were on me as he continued. I was sure every person in that room knew I had this awful secret. They knew I had an abortion. They knew I had been hiding it. The stress sweat gave way to a cold sweat as I convinced myself they could see my own scarlet letter shining brightly. *No, they don't know*, I thought. How could they possibly know? I slowly raised my head up and began to look around discreetly. Had anyone noticed the intense reaction I was having? Could they see the guilt on my face? I had never been very good at hiding my emotions. They must know. This sermon was for me, wasn't it? I looked around again, slowly trying very hard to see who was staring at me. No, no. They don't know. I warred with myself, trying to calm myself down as the pastor continued to talk. No one knew. I knew they didn't know. I knew my secret remained between me and God. As wonderful as all these people were, I was not confident they would understand.

I realized for the first time that I had not dealt with my abortion at all. I had thought when enough time had passed, if I just kept moving forward, it would all kind of work itself out. But what could I do? It was not like there was someone I could talk to about it. Who would understand what I was feeling when I could barely understand it myself? There was no place I could turn to for help like there had been on that fateful day all those years ago. There was no facility here to help me through my post-abortion nightmare. It was all supposed to go back to normal. I was supposed to have the abortion, and life was supposed to resume exactly as it had been before. But it never had. The thoughts that crept up, the emotions that came flooding, the guilt, I pushed them all down and swallowed them as best I could.

I was still in denial of the fact that I had not been helped by that abortion facility. I was still denying that I had to forgive myself and that I was worthy of the forgiveness of others. I still did not know how to get the help and support I needed to move past that experience in my life. Wouldn't it just right itself now that I was living a better life? I left church that day feeling vulnerable, exposed yet affirmed. I managed to escape back to my apartment, completely confident that I could never ever speak about my abortion.

I had been going to a local church with my friend Katie. This was the first solid church I had ever been to and the first place I began to be rooted in sound theology. I had gone to church off and on as I was growing up. Not one of my experiences with the church ever changed who I was. It had no bearing on my daily life. I had never felt any different before, during, or even after the service. The church was where we went to gather occasionally with some members of the community. We would sit through the service, walk outside, and people were acting a mess right after. That was what I thought church was. It was a cultural thing, just something we did. We respected spirituality, but we never applied it to our lives; we were never taught how.

It was at my new church that I learned what theology was.

It was also at my new church that I got baptized. For me, it was such a beautiful process.

On the day I was baptized, I sang an original song I had written called "Jesus, Save My Soul."

When I was finished singing, the prophetic team approached. These were members of the church who were able to encourage those who were being baptized. God had given them a word to speak to me. These are the three prophetic things that stuck with me:

"We are all smiling at each other because we just saw music all around you. Your life will never be without music." This could seem obvious to some, given that I had just finished singing. However, it revealed to me that God was aware of how much I love to sing. It made my heart so happy that music would always be a part of my journey. This prophecy explained that I would have music with me for the long haul, and I was thrilled. God knew this would mean the world to me. The next prophecy that was shared with me I would not fully understand until years down the road.

"The Lord has preserved you for one, and it will be a giving-and-receiving relationship. It's not going to be like the one in the past." This was interesting. I could not say I was blind to men at this point; however, they certainly were not taking center stage within my life as they once had. I did want to get married and was open to dating. It was nice to know that at some point, the right one was going to come along for me.

Lastly, "Your life is like a mosaic, there are all these broken pieces, but God is going to show you the beauty in all of it." Broken pieces? I thought about this for a while. At first, I just assumed that it was because everyone takes journeys in life. No one has a perfect life. There would always be things that are off course. Was that what they meant? Or were they referring to my secret past? Did they somehow know I was hiding something? Was I broken from it? I mulled it over for some time. I knew I did not like thinking about this one too much. It made me uneasy even though they said there was beauty present.

In the months that followed, I learned how to pray, and to pray over others. Prayer was a gift that I had never realized I possessed. Yet, even with all this discovery and growth, I walked around with a victim mentality where my past was concerned. I never shared it with my new friends. If there was one thing Christians could not forgive, it was abortion, right? I maintained silence. It was between me and God, anyway. No one needed to know my secret. Besides, I was doing well, stuffing it in the back of my mind and moving on. No one could deny that. Look how well I was doing. I repeated that to myself in the moments when the guilt and sadness over my abortion threatened to overwhelm me. I was in a new place. I was now a new person. That was in the past, and besides, it was "nothing." Just as the nurse had said on that day all those years ago. I had traveled a far journey to move away from my past, and I had no interest in letting it resurface. I was fine, God loved me, and that was all that mattered.

My faith was grounded, reinforced by many experiences with the Holy Spirit that strengthened it. I would pray, "God, let me encounter someone today that needs you." And as I would walk to work, I would run into someone who looked sad. I would ask if they were ok, and then a conversation would go from there. Being approachable, I realized, was a gift God was granting me. That is the Holy Spirit flowing in me, I realized one day. I did not know why he wanted me to possess this gift, but I accepted it as I did all the things He gave me, with open arms. I had no way of knowing that the Lord was grounding me by giving me these experiences. He was building my trust and strength in him so that I would soon be ready to talk about the darkest parts of my life. He needed me to understand His love and accept the strength He built in me so that I would not feel hurt or shame in sharing my past. Instead, I would know His hand in it, His love, His grace.

CHAPTER 5

The Coffee Shop

I was only a few months from graduation when a friend of mine from my church and I got into a random conversation about my future. He asked me what my plans were when I graduated, and though it was right around the corner, I confessed that I had no plans yet. It was a scary thought to not have a single idea for what my next steps were. He had heard me speak on abstinence before and brought up the fact that he knew of someone who went into schools and spoke to the youth. He thought I would be great at this job. I was flattered by the fact that he reached out to me with this opportunity. I eagerly accepted his offer to put me in touch with a young woman named Melissa, who coincidentally was a member of our church as well. It sounded like an awesome opportunity to be speaking about something I was passionate about as a job!

I met with Melissa at a coffee shop one day to further discuss the opportunity of speaking to the youth on the topic of relationships. The coffee shop was artsy and cozy and filled with a young, college crowd. It was a place I knew well and enjoyed. The place was small with intimate seating within. It was inviting, the kind of place you could sit in for hours. Melissa smiled warmly in greeting, and I could feel the aura of kindness she gave off. She explained that she worked at a local crisis pregnancy center called Amnion. She was the director of the relationship education program. She explained that she shared her story and did her best to reach kids and teens with a message they would not get from our culture. As she spoke, I felt the presence of the Holy Spirit and recognized that this was a divine appointment for something bigger than I could explain. Before the meeting, I had no idea she worked for a pregnancy resource center. I had still never spoken about my abortion, had never shared it with anyone outside of those who went with me on that awful day. My heart began to pound inside me, slamming against my chest as though it were trying to break free. I knew this, again, was the Holy Spirit. My story was welling up inside of me, begging to come out at this moment. Led by the Holy Spirit, I began sharing my past with a veritable stranger. I felt as if things around me had slowed down. I began to speak in small sentences, after which I would examine Melissa's reaction. Her eyes showed empathy, so I continued with a few more sentences. Ever so slowly, I revealed more of my secret to her. The entire time I was waiting for the judgment to come. It didn't. Melissa's calm demeanor encouraged me to be vulnerable. I spoke some more. She listened, the power of my story shining back in raw emotion on her face. I saw no judgment in her eyes. I shared some more. She cast no shame upon me. She listened with true empathy and shocked me at the end by saying, "Do you know how many girls need to hear your story?"

Was that true? This was something I regretted so deeply I lacked the proper words to explain it. We continued to talk. Melissa encouraged me not only to begin speaking on my position with abstinence, but to work to get to the point where I felt comfortable enough to share my abortion story. Was I courageous enough to share my vulnerability? Could I stand up in front of strangers and share a story that I had worked incredibly hard to keep secret?

I had kept this a secret because I believed Christians would NEVER forgive me. They would never be able to understand how I had taken the life of my baby. They would question the kind of person I was. They would say I wasn't worthy of God's forgiveness. But Melissa had done none of those things. She had listened, accepted, and even encouraged me to continue talking to her. She watched my emotions and showed empathetic emotions of her own. At the end, she was encouraging me to share this with others.

This conversation rocked me. Here I had been, for years, operating under the assumption that there was one thing a Christian could never forgive, and Melissa was proving otherwise. I did not need her forgiveness, I knew. I realized though that I very much wanted her acceptance, the acceptance of this stranger who was doing a job I had great respect for, and of a Christian who was a leader to teens and peers alike. I wanted her to accept me and my story without looking down on my past. She had done this. Contrary to what I thought Christians would do, she had accepted me and my story the way God accepted me. This blew my mind.

Maybe there was a reason I came to this exact place to have this conversation with Melissa, who would later because one of my best friends. Just maybe, I really was supposed to share my story with others and possibly help change their minds. I was uncertain. If this was what God wanted of me, of course, I would be willing to do it. At the same time, my emotions were swirling, trying to figure out all the details that would need to have sorted before I could bring my story public. I knew without a doubt though, that before I could share this story with strangers, I needed to share it at home. Confident that my talk with Melissa went well, I packed my things for the weekend and headed out to see my parents.

The reaction my parents had was true to their personalities, the ones I was blind to as a teenager. My father was introspective. He sat unmoving while I spoke with an air of sadness as I came to the worst of it. My mother's reaction was visibly larger. She was horrified. How could I have gone through so much without her knowing? She was upset with herself for not being aware. She had always been a good parent, though now I could see how she felt as though she had failed during that time. They were both resolute in the fact that they never would have wanted me to abort my baby. Both showed forgiveness and overwhelming love immediately following such an emotional conversation.

My mother wrestled with her own emotions over it, though. It was a heartbreaking side effect that I had never envisioned. I know her emotions continued to plague her long after I left that weekend. I can see her emotions clearly and empathize with the unwitting pain I must have caused her by hiding something so big. My sin of my abortion no longer just affected me; it affected my parents because the baby was their grandchild that they would never get to know.

It took a bit of time during that weekend to come to terms with the fact that I had let a lie dictate my actions. Knowing that the abortion clinic had pushed that narrative further home in my mind made me mad. A life-altering decision had been made based on an assumption that was never true in the first place. I had chosen to protect myself, an unstable relationship, and an unknown future over giving life to a precious gift. I realized I was not as "ok" as I thought I was. This was a whole different level of forgiveness that I felt ill-equipped to deal with everyone.

I returned to West Chester feeling the weight of my parents' gracious reaction as a warm hug around me. I was resolved in my path to begin speaking on abstinence to youth, though I was not yet sure I could speak on my abortion. In the span of just a few days, I went from hiding the biggest secret I ever had to being encouraged to share it. Add to that the unveiling of that secret to my parents and all the emotional toil that entailed. There were so many things I felt uncertain about. Could I forgive myself? Could God forgive me? Was I worthy of that forgiveness? Would the friends I'd made these past years be able to look past this awful mistake?

As a part of my training for my new job, I was going to watch Melissa give her talk on abstinence to a group of kids. I could not believe that I, someone who had an abortion, was about to begin getting paid to talk to teens about waiting for marriage to have sex. I was amazed at where I was and at the job I had landed successfully right out of college. I listened to Melissa on that day as she shared her story. I watched the reactions of the kids she spoke to. My story could help change the course of other teens' lives, I realized. Was this God's real purpose for me?

Speaking on abstinence felt like a good step. As I reflected on the path of my own choices, I continued to realize how much I wanted to help other young girls avoid my choices. Advocating for abstinence seemed like a great place to start. I felt God's blessing in this path even while struggling with my own post-abortion emotions, which now seemed to be welling up within me. I had spent so long pushing them down, ignoring them, and swallowing past the lump in my throat when they threatened to boil over. Did I want to face these now? Did I need to move forward? Was it God's intention to have me speak to teens about my abortion?

Emotions and thoughts continued to pop up at random times, and I began to ever so slightly allow those thoughts to sit in my mind for a beat. The more I watched Melissa, and some others whom I worked with who spoke so bravely, the more I felt like I needed to share my experience. I was petrified. I had not dealt with my abortion. I had not allowed myself to think much about it. My perfectly crafted box that held that secret was holding up just fine, wasn't it? Except that I knew that wasn't the case. If someone mentioned the word abortion, I held my breath. I would look around to see if someone was looking at me. Did they know my secret? Was it written on my face? I would slowly exhale when I realized that word hadn't been directed at me. Maybe I had a lot more healing to do where my abortion was concerned. The chief problem being I had no idea where to start.

Fortunately, Melissa knew. She put me in touch with one of our center's counselors, Tina. I was not sure if I wanted to be in a group, so I was thankful no one else showed up to the group counseling session. Here I was, terrified and trying to lay bare the darkest secret I had to a stranger and hoping beyond hope that at the end of it all, there would be peace. Tina was wonderful from the very first moment I met her. Her gentle nature poured over me and immediately set me at ease. I can only hope that every person seeking post-abortion counseling is blessed enough to have such a patient and wise supporter to guide them through the process. That night I began, *"Forgiven and Set Free: A Post-Abortion Bible Study for Women"* by Linda Cochrane. Once again, my life was about to shift.

CHAPTER 6

Healing Is in His Hands

". . . and provide for those who grieve in Zion—to bestow on them a crown of beauty instead of ashes, the oil of joy instead of mourning . . ."—Isaiah 61:3 (New International Version)

efore my counseling, I grieved the loss of my unborn baby, but I also felt thankful. *Thank God I'm not pregnant anymore* or *Thank God I don't have a child now* were thoughts I had continually. I could not imagine my life with a child. I felt grateful that I did not have that responsibility in my life while I had gone to college and grown in the Lord. That made me feel guilty for even thinking about those things. It was a constant warring thought process. A push and pull of what I thought was good and evil. Most days when I allowed myself to think about it, I felt crushed by it.

For the next few weeks, I would be reading through this Bible Study. Each week it would set me up to focus on a different topic. I would read through Scripture, and I would answer questions. These questions were designed to get me to really think through and evaluate myself. I was nervous to begin, but also hopeful.

In the very first chapter of *Forgiven and Set free*, I underlined sentences like "women may attempt to bury their grief," "Relief is the first stage of grieving," "feelings of relief wear off . . . denial begins." *Forgiven and Set Free*, page 15

There was no doubt about it, this was going to be heavy stuff. Even as I pushed forward on that first night of the Post-Abortion Bible Study, I felt overwhelmed. I continued to pray and ask God for the strength I needed to get through this. Strange, huh? Asking God for strength to deal with something that I never should have done in the first place. The overthinking of it was exhausting, and at many times over the next several weeks, I realized how much easier it would be to shut the book and walk away from this whole path. As soon as I thought those things, I knew it was the devil trying to take me off the course God wanted me on for my life.

"Simon, Simon, Satan has asked to sift all of you as wheat. But I have prayed for you, Simon, that your faith may not fail."—Luke 22:31–32

The Bible Study program was intense. Between the readings in the book and the additional counseling sessions, I was in a constant state of heightened emotion. I felt as though I fought myself, my own personal demons, and the devil consistently during this time.

Turning on my emotions after so many years of keeping them turned off where my abortion was concerned was not easy. The first chapter was dedicated to figuring out where I needed healing. Prior to entering a relationship with Christ, I idolized men. I thought that if I could find someone to love me, then I would somehow be validated as a person. I would be worthy, made whole. I reflected on how I had always wanted to wait until marriage to have sex, yet I caved. When Kris went off to college, it was hard for me to have him so far away. I wanted to be closer to him. I worried that I would lose him. Maybe, if we slept together, that would bring us closer and make him want to stay with me. We would have a connection. I had been so insecure in myself and in our relationship. Had he put that pressure on me? Had I put it on myself? I wasn't quite sure. I now had to rethink my teenage emotions and actions with a fine-tooth comb. It was the emotional battle of a lifetime, and it had only been a few days.

In the second chapter, I reflected on who God truly was. I knew this, didn't I? I had been an active Christian for a few years now. Yet, with all the new information I had learned, with the hours of Bible reading I had accomplished, I had not seen God in this light. I knew God would forgive me; I knew he had forgiven me. With the great things that had happened in my life over the past few years, I felt that forgiveness through the favor He granted me. Somehow, I never put together His connection with others. I still felt strongly that other people would not be able to forgive me. That they would constantly look at me as though I were somehow less of a person if they knew I had aborted my child. I failed to view them with God's strength, with God's forgiving power, or God's acceptance. Tina showed me this lesson, especially. As much as I sat there doubting that others could accept and forgive me, she sat there showing me otherwise. She did not judge me. She seemed to accept me just as warmly two weeks into our journey as she had the very first night, I had met her. She had been showing me God's grace in her own actions.

Relief. Denial. Anger. All of these seemed so small but were the emotional equivalent of carrying around a skyscraper building. One by one, I went through Bible, verse after verse, about forgiveness. I answered each question in my workbook. I felt all those emotions one at a time, and then together all at once. For years, I had flung anger at my old best friend and Kris. It festered and mutated into a giant pit of nastiness. I threw my own emotions at them in my mind as I replayed scenarios, cried, and prayed. Forgiving Kris and my old best friend eventually was not so difficult; accepting that I was forgiven by God, difficult. Taking ownership of my actions felt insurmountable. Working through chapter five, "The Need to Forgive," was one of the most difficult weeks in the journey thus far.

By the time I got to chapter six, "Depression," the emotional load I was carrying was not only heavy but raw. The wound was completely ripped open. I felt dizzy with it even as I tried to carry on each day with a smile on my face. The people I encountered around me had no idea I was reliving the most difficult time in my life. They were completely unaware of the broken spirit that I had unburied and was attempting to come to terms with. In the middle of this chapter, one verse felt like a spark of sunlight amidst my very dark days.

"Do not be afraid, you will not be put to shame. Do not fear disgrace; you will not be humiliated. You will forget the shame of your youth and remember no more the reproach of your widowhood. For your Maker is your husband—the Lord Almighty is his name—the Holy One of Israel is your Redeemer; he is called the God of all the earth. The Lord will call you back as if you were a wife deserted and distressed in spirit- a wife who married young, only to be rejected," says your God. "For a brief moment I abandoned you, but with deep compassion, I will bring you back. In a surge of anger, I hid my face from you for a moment, but with everlasting kindness I will have compassion on you," says the Lord your Redeemer."—Isaiah 54:4–8

Redeemer? Yes, He was. If He was the Redeemer, then I could be redeemed. Hadn't I already seen this in my life? Hadn't I already been able to turn my life over to Him and been blessed by the unexpected path my life had taken since I was saved? Yes, I had. I realized this slowly in the sort of slow awakening one has from a very deep and much-needed sleep. Cloudy and a little dazed, I began to realize that God wanted me on this journey. I would only be able to help and inspire others if I knew I was forgiven.

Chapter seven was heartbreaking and oddly freeing. It was amid the studies in this chapter that I had a very vivid dream about the child I had aborted. I had been sitting on my bed, going through my Bible Study when I began to feel tired. I shut my eyes for what I thought would be a moment, and quickly fell asleep. Even now, all these years later, I can recall the dream I had. The images were so vivid, the colors so lifelike.

I was on the landing area at the top of a staircase, on my knees. A little boy, about three or four years old with short cut dark hair was with me. I was hugging him and crying, his small hand gently patting my back. I never saw his face, but I could feel the soothing parts of his hand upon my back. Tears were streaming down my face. He pulls away from me and says, "Mommy, look at all the colors on the ground." I followed his gaze down to the floor. "Look at all the colors on the floor," he said, "look, crimson red!" Immediately, I was reminded of Jesus' blood. I woke up feeling the remnants of tears upon my face. I felt peaceful and oddly happy, though I had clearly been crying. I thought over the dream. I knew in those moments that I had been carrying a little boy, whose name I felt sure was Tyler. Tyler was most assuredly in heaven, as he had referenced "crimson" and had carried with him an air of calming gentleness. How else would he have known at such a tender age to reference something as "crimson?" Jesus had used his blood to wash away my sins, He had granted me forgiveness from both my aborted son, and God. Jesus had sacrificed his blood; his sacrifice had accomplished what God had willed in granting us all forgiveness of our sins. This dream began the process of releasing my guilt; carrying that sin around with me no longer seemed like my only option. Tyler was offering me forgiveness, and letting me know that in God's eyes, there was no longer anything to forgive.

At my next session with my counselor, Tina, I told her about the dream. She shared with me that other women had also shared baby dreams with her. Days later, I was still in shock at that dream. I was in awe that God had chosen to speak to me in this way, so strongly about Tyler. The true healing was beginning to take place, and I could feel the supernatural presence of God that only strengthened how powerful God was in my life. God was speaking directly to me in that dream, and I felt honored by it. I knew that counseling and Bible Study were working, I was healing in a way I had never imagined I had needed.

In the same way God had sent me that dream, He had also sent me Tina. Tina was the tool that got me to open my heart to go through all of this. She took me by the hand and led me. She walked next to me during the worst moments. I had to do all the work, but I wasn't alone. She was God's physical presence during this time. He had empowered her to take me on this journey, and now I was staring at the back end of it, feeling bewildered and light.

Tina had mentioned that some women decided to have a memorial service for their aborted child. I thought this was a lovely idea. I felt excited to honor Tyler, and inherently sad for having to do it all at once. I knew it was the right thing though. His little soul deserved this solemn remembrance. I began planning it by thinking through as many details as I could. Planning the memorial service was yet another difficult thing that I needed to do to find redemption. It reminded me of my regret and guilt, yet I knew this would bring me closer to healing.

It was Tuesday, December 20th, 2005, the day had arrived. I gathered with my supportive group of friends; Melissa, Kate, and Melanie, as well as my counselor, Tina. We walked into my counselor's home with the Violin Concerto by Beethoven softly playing in the background. I could already sense the sweet presence of God. We opened with prayer, and I read scriptures that God placed on my heart to acknowledge the life of Tyler. I began with,

For you formed my inward parts, you knitted me together in my mother's womb.

I praise you, for I am fearfully and wonderfully made. Wonderful are your works, my soul knows it very well. My frame was not hidden from you, when I was being made in secret, intricately woven in the depths of the earth. Your eyes saw my unformed substance, in your book were written, every one of them, the days that were formed for me, when as yet there was none of them. - Psalm 139:13-16 (English Standard Version)

Then using the powerful energy coursing through me, I picked up my guitar and began to sing the song I had written for Tyler.

Dear Lord,

This is my song

For my little one

That's held in Your arms.

So safe, and so secure,

And loved by You.

I wonder how things might have been,

If I had chosen another way.

I bet you'd have my smile,

And my brown eyes.

There's been pain and sorrow.

If I could, I change it all.

The power of your innocent life has changed me.

I thank You Lord

For all you have done.

You've given my unborn child a voice.

Dear Lord,

This is my song

For my little one

That's held in Your arms.

So safe, and so secure,

And loved by You.

I love you, too.

We performed a candle lighting ceremony honoring the innocent life of my baby boy, and could feel the atmosphere in the room shift. The powerful courage I had felt moments before deflated, and sadness swept through me. My counselor, Tina, handed me a white rose. This rose was a representation of Tyler- innocent, white for purity, soft and lovely- the physical embodiment of Tyler's soul. I placed this lone, delicate rose within a beautiful box, as if I were laying him to rest. The room was filled with a heaviness, as tears from deep within me rolled out. With every moment that passed, despite the heavy sadness, there was a peacefulness that was taking over. I remember looking over at my friends and feeling extremely blessed to have my girls by my side on this solemn day. Their friendships had withstood both good and bad, and I felt amazingly privileged to have such strong support from them all.

When asked, all these years later, each of my friends can recall very powerful moments of this memorial service.

When asked about Tyler's memorial service in September 2021, Melanie recounts, "The specific details of that holy time have grown fuzzy. What I remember most, though, is the somber yet peace-filled; presence of God that came into that room as we honored the life of your precious boy. I remember reading the program and thinking about the heartache you must be going through as you mourned the fact that you would never get to hold him on this side of heaven. I felt deep sadness that we would never get to love on that little boy the way best friends get to do. The great deception of abortion had stolen that from us. But at the same time, I remember being in awe of the reality that in Christ, not only was forgiveness possible, but so was the hope of a future eternity with Tyler. I remember the candlelight and how it felt right somehow to grieve together, to cry together, with the shadows dancing, pointing to the Light that promised to heal and restore. Despite the heaviness, I remember being so honored to stand with you in your pain. Your humility in upward confession, your sweet words directed to your son, and the hope that tied it all together was beautiful, sanctifying, and deeply memorable. I remember being so proud of you, my friend, even as my heart ached with yours over your loss."

Kate explains to me how the entire space felt like, "Holy Ground." "I remember," she goes on to say, "at first there was heaviness, heartbrokenness, devastation within the room. This awful pulling of intense sadness that no one could escape surrounded us. As we went through the service, there was this lifting of energy. The heaviness gave way to this beautifully powerful experience of the washing of the water, knowing that Tyler was with Jesus, that Jesus had forgiven you, and that one day you and Tyler would be reunited in Glory. It was one of the most powerful things I have ever experienced. I have chills right now thinking about that day. The experience was like seeing the ashes turn to beauty."

My friend Melissa shared that "it felt so right to do what the rest of the culture refuses to do—acknowledge, grieve, and celebrate the little life that was such a significant loss. At a time in our history where people have abortions, and then stuff their emotions down in the normalization of such an act, it is the right thing for all parties concerned to have this memorial. To give that child what they deserved—a name, a burial, a putting to rest. It was so healing to witness" Melissa recounts. "Not to ignore but to confront the truth of what was real, and to feel that which a mother should feel. Then, to receive the forgiveness God so longs to give each of us. It was all such a picture of redemption. It made the gospel come alive in a way I'd never experienced."

At the time, I was very much deeply entrenched in my own emotions and was not able to realize that the ones around me were experiencing things that also made their faith grow by witnessing my story. That God should use my mistake in such a way still, to this day, leaves me in awe. He turned a terrible disaster into something that spurs biblical change and tangible lessons within whom this story touches.

The memorial was everything I needed it to be. It was the respectful closure of life that was due my son. On this journey, I had to swallow the fact that abortion did not make my circumstances better. The act of abortion had stayed with me and would always be there. My abortion took the life from the one whom I should have protected. I had swallowed the abortion industries' lies. I had to face and accept that the abortion industry did not, in fact, care about women. I would always regret ending the life of my child. I would live with the fact that I had believed the lie that my life was worth more than my child's. The regret would never leave me; it would be an ever-present reminder of the choice I had made. The memorial was the release of my own guilt, and the full acceptance of the forgiveness I needed to move forward.

My abortion will always be with me; it is a part of my journey, I realized. Like so many, I carried the wreckage of that day around with me in life. It altered me in ways I had not realized, in a very negative way, and for a very long time. Now, although I will always feel the wreckage of that choice, I also felt free.

Until this point in time I had not owned what I had done. I had replayed conversations over the years. I had pushed off the blame. I had been angry at my best friend for her immediate reaction. I was broken-hearted because going through the abortion experience had not, as I had hoped, brought me any closer to Kris. I had felt rage within me for Kris. All the times he had mistreated me. All of those, "I'll call you," only to be sitting alone, all night, waiting by the phone for his ring. All the stories about the girls at college. His flirty smile. His final hug goodbye on that awful day. The sonogram nurse who said, "See, it's nothing." The doctor, for not being truthful with me. It all sat within me, and I had used it all as excuses to not accept my own part of the story. My best friend encouraged me to do it. Kris encouraged me to do it. The nurse told me it wasn't a big deal because it was nothing. I had happily chalked that all up in my mind to alleviate the burden of my own wrongdoing. This Bible Study program stopped that all in its tracks.

Looking back now, I do not remember the point in the Bible Study where I realized that I had not quite accepted my own part in my abortion. When I did realize it, that's when my heart began to change. If I could go back in time knowing what I know now, I would have given Tyler life in a heartbeat. Now as I stood before students every day sharing my story, I knew that I was also giving Tyler's life purpose. He was no longer a statistic. I knew God would use my abortion regret and healing to help so many women never take this path. I also knew it would help other women begin to heal. The gifts that God granted me from this point forward were made more tender and precious now that I understood my journey.

CHAPTER 7

Walking with Purpose

"...He has sent me to bind up the brokenhearted..." Isaiah 61:1
(New International Version)

I journeyed for years after my healing not only spiritually but also emotionally and professionally. I continued going to church and being an active part of my church community. I journaled my thoughts, verses that struck me, etc. Journaling really was a powerful thing in my life. It helped me to release all my thoughts, good and bad. It helped me to see how far I came from one point in time to the next. It relaxed me as I was able to throw all my ramped-up energy over different subjects down on paper. My journals reveal the times when it was easy for me to pray and focus, and the times when it was a struggle. Why a struggle? Life. I was an active person socially, with a lot of responsibilities for my job. Just like any other person, I struggled with balancing priorities. When I journal, it helps me to realize when I am losing focus or falling out of balance. It helps pull me back to God's path.

I was nearing the end of my twenties at this point. My career was fulfilling in ways I had never imagined. I continued speaking to the youth. Through the years, I had been promoted to the Director of Amnion's Relationship Education Program. Melissa handed the baton off to me after she got married and began the new chapter of her life. I loved this new position and working for this ministry in general. I learned so much from Melissa and her leadership. She had built a team that was racially diverse with both men and women speakers, which helped us reach a broader youth audience base. I continued to lead the way for our office by getting us into schools that others never thought we would be allowed into. We were speaking in over fifty schools, many of which were very liberal and very socially diverse, not usually known for a pro-life and abstinence message. Some were inner city schools in Philadelphia, and others were exclusive private schools. We had a vast range of socio-economic areas within our travel distance. The messages that we were sharing were significantly more important than the salary we received, and I made sure that the kids knew that we were not there for monetary purposes, as our program was offered to them all for free. Our presentation was two to three days long, depending on the class lengths in each school.

There was something very satisfying about looking out into the faces of those pre-teens and teens. Many of them, I realized, just wanted to be noticed, heard, and valued. The pressures of adolescence are pushing down on them, as they had once pushed down on me.

They watched my entire team with skepticism at first, ready to be bored by yet another school assembly-like presentation. Within a few minutes, we could see their demeanor shift. They realized this was not, in fact, their normal presentation. They realized we were sharing our personal stories, our personal journeys. It never got old doing this presentation repeatedly. Each time was a reminder that I was a part of something that I had very much needed when I was a teen. I was able to be that for them, the very thing that I had lacked during a time where my decisions shifted from easy to life-altering. Our entire team was speaking life into them. We were telling them that they could save sex for marriage. I was telling them the harsh reality of why they should be doing that by using my story as a real example. It was authentic. There was something about being seen as a Black post-abortive woman advocating for abstinence, a young, handsome Spanish guy telling these students that he was waiting for marriage even though it is not popular, that spoke volumes to them. We shared that by respecting their bodies and seeing their worth, they could ultimately experience an authentic relationship that did not have to end in heartache. We could see their minds changing right before us. It was as if they had been longing for someone to tell them that they did not have to proceed on the path that was considered the "norm." We gave them that permission. We supported it. We lived it. We showed them examples of what the outcome for their futures could be if they walked in respectful pursuit of their well-being.

I was also able to share about a short relationship I had after I had committed to saving sex for marriage. This would be the first time that sex was not included in the relationship. We got to know each other better because our purpose was really to get to know each other. In retrospect, I am so grateful for not giving myself to him. When we broke up, I was extremely heartbroken and sad. That is a natural response to any breakup. This relationship was by far the healthiest I had ever been in, but it also revealed areas of my life where I was insecure. There were still things from my past that I contributed to this relationship. The best part is, we didn't take anything from one another that wasn't ours. I left this relationship whole because men were no longer my foundation, Jesus was. A breakup can be healthy even in sorrow. I was learning to trust that God only wanted to give me what was best for me. As time passed, it was clear that this relationship was not what was best for me or for him.

When I shared this experience with the students, it showed them that I was living out the very concepts I was teaching them.

As our small group traveled from school to school, we got to witness teens becoming empowered. The more we spoke, the more rewarded we felt that our message was getting through. Positive feedback followed us on our journey, which is what I believed helped pave our way into new schools. It was a time of great growth for my entire team, and our ministry.

In my social life during this time, I watched as my friends coupled off. It happened over a period of years, but in the moment, it sometimes felt like they all jumped into marriage simultaneously. My former boyfriend was even married. While I was lucky enough to be surrounded by people who never ever made me feel excluded or awkward for my single status, I nevertheless struggled with it.

I prayed often to God about it. I sought God's advice on what I needed to do to find a husband. I felt I had made the changes God called me to make. I focused on what I thought He would want of me. Still, my husband did not come. I longed for children, for a family of my own, for a best friend to walk through life with. That easy, back-and-forth exchange that comes to people who had known one another intimately for so long and consequently move in harmony through the world, I wanted that. I felt ready for it. God's time is a funny thing, though. It's very easy to say that we accept things when God wants them for us; it's an entirely different thing to wait it out when you feel so confidently that you are ready.

One of my journal entries from this time reads, "I really am longing for my husband to come. I really want to get married and have precious kids that I can raise in Your name. Everyone around me seems to be married & has kids. I really want to share my life with one person. I do not want to choose because I am not very good at it. In the meantime, help me to be secure where I am at." In many ways, it was a terribly romantic notion, the stuff of movies. But I had seen this in action. I had seen it happen all around me, and I was eager to count myself among those equally blessed.

In the past, I had dated. It felt like random dating though, and while now it was more chaste than anything I had done in my high school or college years, it still sometimes felt a bit haphazard. Dating, I learned, should be done with a purpose. It was not just about who looked good to you in the moment, or whom you were attracted to. Although those things played a part, they were not the only factors. What did the other person value? What were their faith views; did they align with my own? I knew I needed to date someone with views that aligned with mine because my faith was an intricate part of who I was. It was the root of who I was. Those around me needed to support that and feed it so that it grew and never diminished, the way I would with them. Were our life and world beliefs in line? These things were at the forefront of my mind as far as dating went. I have never, in my teen or early college years, even considered dating with a purpose in this way.

For quite some time while in college and even after I graduated, I moved out of my apartment, and I had the opportunity of living with a wonderful family from my church. I knew they were a great family before I moved in with them. They were the epitome of kindness, generosity, and good, old-fashioned family values from the moment I was introduced to them. Living with them though, I learned so much that I had never known I wanted to know.

When I moved in with this family, I got to witness a relationship that was biblically bound together in a way I had never thought to consider. In the normal course of a day, I would watch their interaction with one another, with their children. I watched conflict spur and resolutions occur in a very graceful way. They were not perfect, but they showed me what it was like to raise a godly family. The wife stayed home with the kids; she homeschooled them. It seemed often that every moment of their day was alive with educational moments. I was amazed at how effortless she made it seem. It was inspiring to see children growing up in a healthy environment. I wanted this for my future. The husband loved his wife so well. Not just by saying, "I love you," but rather by acts of kindness and love that he did for her and for the entire family effortlessly. I wanted that. I lived with them for years, and through it all I remained steadfast in the hope that I could one day enjoy a relationship as lovely as this one. I felt hopeful that the changes I was making within would help me reach that point. God once again was showing me examples of Him here on earth.

When I thought back to my younger relationships, I was always in pursuit. I was finally in a place where I was willing to wait for what God had for me. When the time was right, the right person would come to me. In the meantime, my life was going to be spent chasing God. I resolved myself to a new focus. I prayed a lot and decided to use my single time to the advantage of others. I filled the hours of my life in service to God in every way I could think of. Having a purpose was important to me. I liked goals and thrived on setting the details of those goals. Not big goals, mind you . . . not the ones like, "I will be married by twenty-nine." Instead, I set goals for work. I joined groups that were working toward things. I was busy and thriving and beginning to see that I was perfectly ok on my own.

Christ was wholly my foundation; not my ex-boyfriend, or men in general; not the distractions of partying, and late nights out; not the physical act of love, which is so often confused as real love. Christ was the foundation of my world. I was complete and strong in Him, and because of that, I knew that I was utterly resplendent on my own. During this time, I learned my worth. I learned my value. I reflected on my past journals and saw growth. I knew that God continued to have a plan for me, and the power in that truth was amazing.

I was on a mission trip coming back from Israel and I was thinking over all the things God had done thus far in my life that I suddenly became overwhelmed with thankfulness. I remember praying, *Thank you, God. I could die today, and I would be completely satisfied because I am so thankful for the life you have given me these past years that have been yours.* I was made anew, refreshed, and reset on the journey I had been on. Every step of my life for years had been on the path that God had intended for me. It was a feeling of complete surrender and trust that brought so much peace to my heart. God had placed my feet on a solid foundation that could not be shaken.

"Therefore, who hears these words of mine and puts them into practice is like a wise man who built his house on the rock. The rain came down, the streams rose, and the winds blew and beat against that house, yet it did not fall because it had its foundation on the rock. But everyone who hears these words of mine and does not put them into practice is like a foolish man who built his house on sand. The rain came down, the streams rose, and the winds blew and beat against that house, and it fell with a great crash." —Matthew 7:24–27

CHAPTER 8

Dismantling the Lies, and an Unexpected Encounter

In the course of my work at Amnion Crisis Pregnancy Center, I realized that I had never learned the anatomy of a fetus. I had taken health classes, I had taken science classes, and yet I had never learned about the fetal development that took place in pregnancy. Seemed like such a strange thing to have gotten through school without learning.

No wonder it was so easy for me to see abortion as a viable path for myself during a time when I was cloaked in fear. I had been woefully undereducated about the development of a fetus. It was "nothing" as the nurse in the abortion clinic had told me on that awful day. If I had only understood that *"For you created my inmost, being you knit me together in my mother's womb." (Psalm 139:13)*

Or that at the time of my visit to that abortion facility, my baby was about the size of a blueberry with its nostrils, mouth, eyes, and ears becoming more defined. *It's nothing,* I can still hear the nurse say. While my anger at the nurse had healed, it was replaced by a mounting heat at the injustice we were doing as a society. That nurse knew that it was more than nothing at that stage of development. She knew, but she had been trained well by an organization that hid its prejudice behind the mask of healthcare. By an organization who sold fetal body parts and fetal tissue in the name of "science."[3]

I was learning more about Planned Parenthood and its target of the Black community. I had no idea at that time that abortion ended 360 Black lives every single day.[4] This is modern-day genocide. In New York City more Black babies have been aborted than born alive. Why wasn't anyone talking about this? I continued to research only to learn that this was all a part of a carefully calculated and strategic plan by Planned Parenthood founder, Margaret Sanger, and her partners to target the Black population.[5]

Sanger was supposedly an advocate for women's rights; hadn't I learned that in school? She was someone I should look up to who had helped bring health care into areas where it had not been before, wasn't she? The more research I did for my job, the more I was horrified at what I uncovered. She was a eugenicist that stated, "We don't want word to get out that we want to exterminate the Negro population."[6] Planned Parenthood is promoted as an organization that exist to help people,

3   David Daleiden, "University of Pittsburgh Won't Explain its Planned Parenthood Ties," Newsweek, 5/26/21, https://www.newsweek.com/university-pittsburgh-wont-explain-its-planned-parenthood-ties-opinion-1594564

4   Ryan S Bomberger, "Politifact Aborts the Facts about Abortion being the leading killer of Black Lives," Radiance Foundation, 4/2/18, https://www.theradiancefoundation.org/theleadingkiller/

5   Kay C James, "Even with Removing Margaret Sanger's Name, Planned Parenthood Is Still Influenced by Racist Founder," The Heritage Foundation, 7/29/20, https://www.heritage.org/life/commentary/even-removing-margaret-sangers-name-planned-parenthood-still-influenced-racist

6   John J Conley, "Margaret Sanger was a eugenicist. Why are we still celebrating her?", America: The Jesuit Review, 11/27/2017, https://www.americamagazine.org/politics-society/2017/11/27/margaret-sanger-was-eugenicist-why-are-we-still-celebrating-her

to educate people, to help teens feel safe. That is what I had grown to believe well into my teenage years. How had I not realized that Planned Parenthood facilities were strategically located in low-income, minority areas? There had to be more to this.

There was. So much more. I uncovered that Black women were five times more likely to have an abortion than White women. I learned that the number one killer in the Black community was not Black-on-Black crime, not guns, drugs, heart disease, or even cancer. It is the direct and intentional killing of a human life inside the Black woman's womb.[7] I will never forget when I heard the powerful words of Pastor Clenard Childress,

"The most dangerous place for an unarmed Black person to be is in the womb of their Black mother."

I could not deny that Planned Parenthood had been incredibly clever in their language. They use words like health care, family planning, reproductive act, and a woman's right to choose. Many of these phrases sounded empowering. They gave off the aura of independence, trustworthiness. They played at the emotional strings that each phrase wrought. If you only looked surface deep, this was a fantastic organization. I know I had believed that when I was younger. These emotionally triggering phrases do a great job of hiding the fact that this company stands for death. They cover up the fact that their original intentions were to destroy the Black population by convincing us to kill off our own children. They mistakenly believed this kept their hands clean, since it was an individual's choice that led them to the door of death.

When I first began to open my eyes to Planned Parenthood, I had absolutely no idea that this would eventually lead me to begin my path as a pro-life activist. It was years of learning more, talking to people, and

---

7   Ryan Bomberger, 2018.

hearing stories before I would take up my charge to fight for life. Not because I needed that long to be angered enough to do something, but because I did not know where to start to effect change at that time. That all came later. The courage to do it, however, was being built within me at this time. When God's hand is on you, and He has called you for a purpose in something, there is an anointing that falls on you. God is saying, "This is why I created you, and you are walking in it now, finally." There were still bricks He needed to lay within me and around me for me to live this out. It all came together, years later in His time. We are all created to glorify God. Our journeys in life provide the unique skills and opportunities we need to accomplish this in the way He designs. We glorify Him when we do what it is He has called us to do.

I will never forget when I got to attend the Bound4Life Conference with Pro-Life Advocate Lou Engle in Washington DC. Lou asked women like me, who had abortions and now regretted their decision, to come up onto the stage. I joined about thirty other women on stage that day. Lou began to pray as three hundred of us filled the room with our energy. He prayed that God would give us the boldness to speak out against the very thing we had done. He prayed we would bring healing and hope to others. I sobbed. I knew even as a newbie in my walk with Jesus, that God was calling me to this purpose. As Lou finished up his prayer, I felt a hand gently rub my back. When the prayer ended, I turned around and saw that it was Norma McCorvey. She looked me in the eyes and said, "God is going to use your story in a powerful way." When she hugged me, it was like I could feel her years of pain and regret but there was a sense of freedom, too. This was Norma McCorvey a.k.a., Jane Roe from Roe v. Wade. After that law was passed, Norma is quoted as saying, "I am dedicated to spending the rest of my life undoing the law that bears my name" (Norma McCorvey 9-22-1947-2-18-2017). In that moment, this famous stranger spent a moment of solidarity in our mutual regret of decisions gone wrong. We carried that regret with us, and both sought to right the wrong in whatever way we could now that we knew better. She was a kindred spirit with us all; I recognized it in our meeting. This was a powerful moment for me, further hitting home the fact that God was calling me to reach others about abortion. He needed me to use my story. Was I doing enough already or was He calling me to more action? Only He knew the answer to that question. I just needed to be ready to follow.

Having been through the intense healing I had gone through also helped me on my journey for years to come. Many things came to a head for me as I became wiser and more in tune with the needs of those around me. I had been incredibly blessed in my support system since I stepped foot in that first Campus Crusades meeting in college. It was the individual people around me, not the organizations, that supported me through my most difficult times.

I have been fortunate enough to have been involved in some fantastic churches who have wholeheartedly affected positive change in many ways throughout their communities and the world. One place that seems to consistently fall short is the post-abortive outreach. We all want to advocate for life but sometimes forget the people who had not received that message in time. They sit, as I had, hiding in their pew, praying that no one would learn their secret. They sit believing that abortion is the one sin Christian people cannot forgive. They sit alone, buried under guilt, feeling worthless and unworthy. They want to heal and have no idea where to start and are too afraid to approach the leaders among them that should greet them with compassion. As I continue to walk my journey, this is an area I am working on. Helping churches and church leaders understand the necessary part they can and should play in helping to bring healing to the post-abortive women and men is a part of my goal. Both men and women alike are walking around with a heaviness that many cannot understand. Forgiveness and support can help them on their path to finding their own healing.

When a woman calls us hours away from her abortion appointment, and we help change her mind, there is support. Pregnancy Resource Centers existed to help that mother with her needs. From baby gear to babysitting to help so that they can finish school or learn a trade, those supportive services are out there. As Christian organizations, it's our responsibility to know how to speak to these women, how to put them in touch with the services they need, and how to support them for as long as they may need that support. Equally as Christian organizations, it's our responsibility to know that there are those walking among us broken from the life they did not protect. Broken because they believed that a quick abortion would bring normalcy to their life once more, only to discover the nearly unbearable guilt that now walks within them constantly, the embarrassment of their actions, the shame of it all, the unworthiness they feel pushing upon them daily. We should know how to reach these people. We should all know how to tell them that we see them, that we can forgive them as God can. We should know about support groups and counseling services that can help them find the healing they need. Most importantly, we should know how to hear their story with compassion and empathy, showing them the gifts God has given us all to take care of one another.

After I was saved, I knew God had forgiven me. I knew that God loved me. The problem was I did not believe the same of the people around me. I was worried about their thoughts, how they would react, how they would not accept me any longer once they knew. I figured I would just keep it between me and Jesus. I did not realize how much that was affecting me in ways that I did not understand. Knowing that now, and speaking that into other leaders, it is my hope that we can reach those among us who are feeling the same as I had.

This is what I spent my time learning while I waited for my future to show up. I grew stronger with each month that passed. I felt a confidence in my independence that I had never had before. I felt free from the past inadequacies that plagued me. A contentment now sat where longing had once been. God could take me to Him tomorrow, and I felt peaceful that I was living my life entirely cloaked in His glory.

CHAPTER 9

He Makes All Things New

"Forget the former things; do not dwell on the past. See, I am doing a new thing." -- Isaiah 43:18-19

I t's early October 2008 when I am just getting into bed. I snuggled down and flipped open my laptop to check my emails. I saw a notification email from Facebook that I had a new friend request. I click the email open and there it is. I see the name and my heart starts to slam in my chest. My adrenaline kicked in, my heart responding with a frenzied thump. The beating grew louder as I stared at the screen. No way. Come on. Why in the world? This can't be right. I closed the laptop. Did I just see that right? I opened the laptop again and clicked into the email. WHAT? Come on. No way. The incessantly silly questions continued for what felt like hours. I am ignoring this. Absolutely NOT going to even acknowledge it. Then, I accepted his friend request. I sat there, the frantic beating of my heart the only noise as I took deep breaths trying to calm down. *Ok, God. I don't know what this is about but lead me*, I thought. I clicked into my email, followed the notification, and found myself on Facebook, reading a message that said,

> I know we haven't spoken to each other in years but there's some things that I need to tell you. I'm a Christian. My life has changed and the things that I want to say to you I would rather not say over the internet. I'd rather say it to you face to face.

WHAT IS HAPPENING? I wanted to yell. I processed for a hot minute before I scrambled over to his Facebook page to see what information I could find. No picture of course, which I had already noticed. PA Adult and Teen Challenge, ok. I had heard of that organization. They helped both teens and adults battling addictions. No other useful information was on his profile. Back to the message I went. He dropped in some more information, pointing to how he had changed his life, which I read over. My eyes kept returning to his name, Kris McFadden. Can't be. It can't be . . . I read it. I saw it, and yet I couldn't swallow it down. After all these years, poof, he just pops up!

I tossed and turned all night. I told our story all the time. Had my retelling of it somehow brought him back around? Why would he want to talk? What could he possibly have to say after all these years? Then it hit me. I had been telling my story for years. It was my own journey, my own pain, my own lessons learned, and my own recounting of how I had grown in those things. It wasn't his story. Maybe he had his own story to tell, and for some reason, he wanted to tell that story to me.

I got to work the next day, still reeling. I was still in a state of shock! I informed some of my co-workers who all sat outwardly portraying the absolute shock I felt. I just could not function. I kept shouting at them, "What is happening?" "What is God doing?" I stuttered over my own words. I, a person who made her living by publicly speaking her own story, was stammering to put sentences together as my brain tried to process "The return of Kris McFadden." Hours after his initial friend request, and the shock was still rocking through me. Later that week when I had to give my talk to a new group of teens, I froze. This was a talk I had given probably hundreds of times by this point. Halfway through my presentation, I began to stumble and bumble; it was like I had absolutely no idea what I was talking about. I knew my own story backward and forward. I was so familiar with it after all these years that I could give this presentation in my sleep. Yet, Kris's reentry into my life had completely rocked my world. I somehow made it through the day, swearing to myself that I would get it together.

My walls were up. There was no question that I had very little trust in the fact that this would be anything other than the same old song and dance we had done in high school. You know the one . . . "I'll call you." And then you wait by the phone for his call. You finally get tired of waiting and call him only to hear, "Kris isn't home right now, I'll let him know you called." Then you sit there and replay the "I'll be home tonight and call you" conversation you had with him mere hours earlier. We had done that dance transitioning from his senior year of high school into his freshman year of college. I had waited, like a good girlfriend should. He was hesitant because he was in college and wanted to explore the world, or more specifically, the girls in it. I had done everything I could think of to keep his attention and affections for months, including giving him my virginity. He played coy games; he dazzled me with his smile. I had chased and chased him. He seemed to enjoy keeping me running after him. He had never turned to chase me. It had taken me years to realize that he hadn't respected me. He hadn't respected himself. Neither of us had the first inclination back then of how to do that. That was only a lesson I had learned with time and healing. Was this someone I wanted to reenter into my life after all the work I had done to get right with the Lord? To get right with myself.

When I could get my emotions under control, I knew there was a reason for this. I knew God had a plan. I just was not sure if that plan was testing me to see if I would fall into old ways, or if God had brought the same healing to Kris's life, and I somehow played a part in that now.

I finally calmed down enough to answer his message. We chatted back and forth, and I agreed to give him my number. I would not say that my responses were friendly. Cordial, sure. I had a great life now; his name brought back everything I had once been, every toxic thing we had been to each other.

I knew though that I had to let him know I was not the same person. Ironically, he seemed to be trying to tell me that he wasn't the same person either. Still, I doubted. I waited for the games to begin. A few weeks into our talking, and the games had yet to appear. What did appear was a very interesting man who had traveled quite a long journey. He would say things like, "The longer you know me, the more you will see you can trust me." In our conversations, he was confident, steady, and calm. This was the exact opposite of the guy I had known all those years ago.

We talked for a few weeks before I agreed to meet him in person. We chose an Italian restaurant that was close to where I lived. I was surprised to see that he was already there when I arrived. The nerves rocked through me, even as I was conscious of the fact that he too must feel nervous. He was sitting down when I walked in. The journey I had taken, finding forgiveness, and forgiving him, was taken to a new level in that moment. He wasn't just the character in the teenage story I shared with others. He was a real, tangible person in my life at this moment. Maybe that lasted and maybe he flitted out of it as fast as he had jumped in, but in that moment, the realization of the journey we had both traveled separately seemed deeply significant. I sat across from him, knowing that somehow, we had traveled a separate road that led us both to a path set passionately upon Christ. Before he even said a word, his presence made it clear that he was a different person. He had this light, this gentleness that settled him into a place I had never seen him in.

We made small chit chat until the moment came when he shocked me by saying, "I wanted you to know that the reason I ended our relationship, which was a very childish thing to do, was because I didn't want to face the fact that we ended the life of our baby."

Here was this big man, a masculine entity that no longer looked around the world with teenage arrogance, but instead made the room stand still within his calming presence, confessing to his weakness from years ago. It was the first time I realized that abortion affected men. I was shocked to not only hear this but also to realize the effect it had on him. My Christian faith taught me that men were called to lead and to protect. He had not done those things all those years ago, comprehension for his own emotions growing within me.

While I had been going through college and evolving in my faith, Kris had been battling his demons with addiction. His battle, thankfully, led him to Teen Challenge. Teen Challenge was where Kris found his faith and sobriety.

On New Year's Eve 2006, right before the ball dropped, Kris went into a small chapel by himself at Teen Challenge in Pittsburg, PA and began reading through Romans 1:28–32. It was the powerful truth in those verses that revealed everything he was apart from Christ. The Holy Spirit in that moment helped him to understand his need for God. Everything from his past and even up to this point hit him like a ton of bricks. In that tiny chapel at the start of 2007, he surrendered his life to Jesus. Only after that could he make things right with the people he had hurt. I was one of the first people that God put on his heart to apologize to after he strengthened his relationship with God.

I went home that night certain of only a few things. One, Kris had transformed as I had. Two, everything I had been building and rebuilding seemed to be coming into place for this moment in time. Three, I was terrified.

He began calling me every day after that. I was conflicted. I would be nice, then mean. My emotions were everywhere, and I kept waiting for things to revert to what they had been nine years before. Kris was consistent though, pursuing me with purpose. We did not live close to one another, and the distance helped to move things slowly. He never wavered with the distance. He was steadfast through my emotional peaks and valleys. We had somehow switched roles. I had become the one who did not wait around for the phone calls. I went about my life, and if it lined up that I was home to chat, then we did. If it did not, then I was ok with that. Kris, through it all, made it clear he was not going anywhere. He stood resolute in his pursuit, allowing me to see that he truly was transformed in the Lord. The remnants of who he had been nowhere to be found, and it became inherently clear as the days went by.

I knew God wanted me to stop being afraid. I knew I needed to take a leap of faith when Kris asked me point blank if I wanted us to be together. I told him I was scared but said yes. A few weeks later, a visit with his mom showed me I was listening to God correctly, again. He glowed about me to his mom. He had never ever done anything like that in our past. He sat unabashedly as he said, "See, isn't she amazing?" His mom affirmed his thoughts, and I sat there shocked by it all. *This is how every girl should feel*, I thought. Things weren't perfect, but he only had eyes for me. He thought I was the best thing in the world! I could not deny that he was what I had been praying for.

Over the next few weeks, our relationship continued to deepen. He would travel to me on the weekends and stay at my friend's house. We both remained committed to waiting to have sex until marriage. That was extremely important for both of us. Though we remained firm in honoring each other with our purity, this was a test for us both. We even hit a point in our courtship where we stopped kissing all together, to lessen the temptation to be intimate. Our relationship was different in every aspect this time around. In our teenage years, physical attraction was a leading motivation to our entire relationship. Now, there was a depth that I had never known could exist between us. The foundation of who we were as individuals rested firmly in God; therefore, the foundation of our relationship was rooted in God as well. We discussed things with each other that were philosophical and ethical. We shared our goals and dreams. We shared adventures we had, lessons we learned, and asked each other difficult questions to ensure that our connection was founded on principles. We each wanted a true partnership from the other. The days of fleeting physical attraction were over and ushered in the roots of a deeply grounded tree. Our roots continued to entwine and wrap around one another, preparing us for our future.

A little over two months after our first initial contact, we found each other on New Year's Eve. He took me out to dinner at Penn's Landing, in Philadelphia, Pennsylvania. Just before midnight, we stepped outside to watch the fireworks display. Kris stood behind me as the sky lit up with gorgeous color. As it came to an end, I turned to find him kneeling. Tears immediately started to stream down my face. Our entire relationship, from high school to now flashed before my eyes. I could not believe Kris McFadden was asking me to be his wife. His words faded into a beautiful symphony when he placed my beautiful engagement ring on my finger, after hearing my emotional, yes to marry him. In that moment, the fear, doubts, and confusion all disappeared. I saw only him. I felt only happiness and peace within. I could not believe that God did this for us. I felt like our story was too good to be true. I went to bed that night too excited to sleep. All I could do was stare at my ring, smile, and thank God for His faithfulness.

I remember returning to speak at a school where I had been doing my presentation for years. Some of these teachers had heard my talk dozens of times before. Only on this day, the talk was different. I could announce that Kris had come back into my life, and that we were in fact engaged to be married that coming spring. The teachers' reactions were priceless, and the teens' expressions seemed to heighten with a renewed sense of hope. My abortion story and healing had been a powerful one. Many teens had shared with me the impact my life had made on them. The impact became deeper when Kris and I were brought full circle to one another again.

Our wedding date was set for June 27th, just eight months after our initial reconnection. Kris had asked my father for my hand in marriage, which I thought reflected the respect he had learned in his own journey. It awed me. We were so committed to building a strong foundation that we wanted to do everything in a pragmatic way. We had both seen examples of the way things could be done that were not necessarily in keeping with the way God desired for those things to happen. Even though sometimes that worked out for people, we did not wish to do things according to any other way than the Lord's. We did not live with one another before we got married. We fought temptation and did not sleep with one another before we said our vows. We knew this was a more traditional, old-world way of proceeding. We loved that idea. We both believed it set us up for a biblical foundation for our future.

We had discussed the details of what we wanted very carefully as most engaged couples do. I thought over my journey and wanted to be surrounded by those that knew where I had come from, supported me through my journey, and were invested in seeing the best for my future, as I was to them all. My bridal party was filled with women who had impacted my walk with God as well as with Kris. Melissa was my Matron of Honor. Katie, my earlier mentor, Melanie, and Kate were all a part of my special day. All the women in my bridal party and those who helped make our wedding day exactly how we imagined, had walked my healing journey with me. They had shared laughter, tears, and adventure. They had watched me struggle with being single, they had helped heal my broken heart, and they had cheered me on in life. All my obedience to God, all the challenges to understand the Bible and its teachings, to receive God's word, it all came together to form this moment in time.

My soul sister, Monica, whom I had met on my very first mission trip, used her beautiful voice to guide me down the aisle. Her voice flooded the simple chapel, reaching the finespun, draped white tulle above and floating around us like the delicate petals of the gerbera daisies I held tightly in my hands. Around two hundred people joined us, filling the air with wondrous love and support as my father gently walked me down the aisle. I could hear the sniffles and was vaguely aware of the tissues being passed as emotions swept us all away to new heights of love. Monica's voice sang "He's Always Been Faithful" by Sara Groves.

Her voice became emotional as she watched me walk done the aisle because she knew what this song meant to me. She had been by my side for years, knowing that the culmination of such a difficult journey was ending with the reunification of Kris and I brought about powerful emotions in us all.

Our ceremony consisted of common marriage ceremony rituals as well as a few we added in so that we could firmly keep our vows rooted in spirituality. We had incorporated a washing of the feet. There was something amazingly powerful seeing Kris on his knees, in his suit, washing my feet. I felt that same power rock through me as I shuffled down onto my knees in my flowing white gown to do the same to him. The demonstration of washing one another's feet portrayed the love of serving each other. The Spirit fully present in the room, granting a transfer of energy within us, and to those all around us. It felt as though we had opened the ceiling to let the intense rays of the sun bear down on us all. When it came time for our vows, we spoke from the heart. Kris promised to be a covenant keeper as God is a covenant keeper to us all. The promise meant that he would never leave me, that he was committed to me. Because of our past together, because he had needed to run away from me to hide from the guilt he felt, this was a significant vow. He wanted me and everyone else to know that no matter what came, he would remain steadfast, just as God was steadfast to us all. It was ironic because my favorite vow to him was similar. Though the storms come raging, I am committed to never letting go. We needed one another to know this of us. We both needed to express that the foundation of our love would not be shattered, regardless of whatever life threw at us.

When it came time to light our unity candle, we followed it by lighting a memorial candle for Tyler. This was a special moment for us. In our wedding program we let our guest know that this was to honor our unborn baby's life. Kris and I both knew that our story would impact so many lives. Tyler would always be a part of it. Holding hands, we stood and remembered him together, with our supportive community surrounding us. We knew our wedding day was just the beginning.

Before we knew it, God was blessing us yet again, with a child. This beautiful life was a gift to us in so many profound ways. Only God could have written a story like this. Healing our individual broken pieces and remaking us whole in His image again. Then setting us on a pathway toward one another could only have happened with God leading us. Our wedding will always be a reminder of what the hand of God can do. He redeemed two lost souls, healed our pasts, and brought us back together for His purposes. I knew our wedding day was just the beginning of His redemption in our journey as one. I will forever be grateful for a God who does not waste anything when we are willing to surrender all to Him. He is the only One that can take our pain and make something absolutely beautiful out of it. He is an amazing God who redeems!

"I have swept away your offenses like a cloud, your sins like the morning mist. Return to me, for I have redeemed you." --Isaiah 44:22

EPILOGUE

T his epilogue is for those considering abortion and all those sitting painfully on the other side. I've been where you are, and I speak directly to you now.

To those considering abortion,

I see your fear, you are not alone in it.

If I could be there to hold your hand, I would.

This rough time is but a small moment of your entire life, do not make this decision thinking only of the immediate.

You ARE strong enough to carry this baby.

Yes, it is unconventional, and at times, downright terrifying, but beauty will come through on the other side.

The abortion industry lies.

The people on the other end of that phone do not care about you. They do not care that you are scared, vulnerable.

The quick fix to your "problem" that you seek is how they make their money; that is all they see.

Abortion will never be normal, and things will never go back to "normal."

Abortion will never make your circumstance better.

Abortion will take the life from the one whom you should protect within you.

The regret will never leave you.

Please know that the child in your womb is innocent and is uniquely created.

Please choose life for your baby, your only choice is to not end the life of your child.

Choosing to parent or giving your baby to a loving family that cannot conceive is such an amazing gift.

We deserve better than abortion.

You can do this!

To all of those sitting painfully on the other side of abortion,

The trauma of abortion will not magically disappear.

There is nothing normal or natural about ending the life of an innocent baby in the womb.

It changes you.

However, there is a Savior who is willing to take on your mistakes by His death and resurrection and *make you new!*

When you surrender it all to God, He alone can turn it all around for good.

You will heal.

The death and resurrection of Jesus Christ is enough to take on your sin.

Regret will hit you like a ton of bricks.

You will weep.

You will question how you could have done such a thing.

You will mourn.

Through Christ you heart will be set free.

Your new life in Christ will terrify the enemy.

When the war comes raging against you, keep close to God's heart. That is the safest place to be.

God will use all your brokenness.

One day, you will meet your baby/babies in heaven.

There is nothing God cannot redeem!